Social Psychology in
Cross-Cultural Perspective

Social Psychology in Cross-Cultural Perspective

Fathali M. Moghaddam
Georgetown University

Donald M. Taylor
McGill University

and

Stephen C. Wright
University of California, Santa Cruz

W. H. Freeman and Company
New York

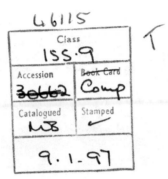
Library of Congress Cataloging-in-Publication Data

Moghaddam, Fathali M.
    Social psychology in cross-cultural perspective / Fathali M.
Moghaddam, Donald M. Taylor, Stephen C. Wright.
        p. cm.
    Includes bibliographical references (p.) and index.
    ISBN 0-7167-2354-9 (cloth).—ISBN 0-7167-2355-7 (paper)
    1. Social psychology—Cross-cultural studies. I. Taylor, Donald
M. II. Wright, Stephen C. III. Title.
HM251.M585 1992
302—dc20   92-23851
                                                         CIP

1 2 3 4 5 6 7 8 9 0 VB 9 9 8 7 6 5 4 3 2

Contents

Preface

A cross-cultural perspective can enrich our understanding of classic and current research in the most important topics in the science of social behavior, including social cognition, social influence, and social relations. Our book is intended to introduce this perspective in social science classes, such as social psychology and organizational behavior, where human social behavior is a focus. We have attempted to write a book that would serve as an engaging supplement to expand the standard "monocultural" review of social behavior offered in introductory courses.

It is often said that books reflect the lives of their authors. In our case, the origins of this book may be found in our work as social psychologists who have experienced a variety of different cultures: Iranian society in the throes of revolution and war; villagers in India grappling with the challenges of poverty and overpopulation; illiterate peasants pouring into newly industrialized cities in South-

East Asia; isolated populations of native peoples struggling to maintain their traditional ways of life in the face of pressures to "modernize" in Northern Canada; recent immigrants and refugees who continue to throng to the United States; ethnic ghettoes in major urban centers in North America and Europe; employees of multinational corporations adapting to radical changes in corporate culture; and of course the students we have taught in our classrooms—a population which was once almost exclusively white and male, but which is becoming increasingly diverse in terms of gender, ethnicity, language, and cultural background. Each of these experiences has helped to shape this book.

An equally important influence on this book has been the traditional training each of us has received, one in Europe and the other two in North America, as social psychologists. In writing this book, this training has led us to reconsider both classic works and the more contemporary research in social psychology with a sincere appreciation for the experimental rigor and methodological sophistication of the investigators. However, we point out how adopting a cross-cultural perspective can allow social psychologists to make more *accurate* generalizations about human behavior.

Our views have been shaped by the times in which we live, an era in which cultural diversity plays an increasingly important role in local, national, and international affairs. As a result of such factors as the collapse of Communism, the internationalization of trade, and the spread of modern communications, the world seems to be shrinking into a "global village." On the other hand, there is also a worldwide "revival" of separatist movements and ethnic consciousness, such as in the splintering of the former Communist states. Throughout our "global village," multiculturalism is becoming stronger and cultural diversity is increasing. Therefore, any serious survey of social behavior in multicultural societies must adopt a cross-cultural perspective.

We have also been influenced by many other researchers in the field. Among these, we would like to thank particularly those who gave valuable comments on earlier drafts of chapters: George Cvetkovich, Wallace Lambert, Robert Serpell, Tod Sloan, and Daniel Robinson. From the initial step of this project, Jonathan Cobb challenged and inspired us by his knowledgeable and skillfully introduced editorial feedback, and the positive features of this book owe a great deal to his craftsmanship.

1

Culture and Social Psychology

A group of blind beggars was traveling together and exchanging stories about all the strange animals they had encountered. One of them said that the next town they would reach had a reputation for being a home to the strangest animal on earth, the elephant. Since none of them had ever come across an elephant before, they agreed that they would go their separate ways and search the town to find an elephant. When night fell, the beggars gathered at their appointed place and each related his experiences. One of the blind beggars, who had touched the elephant's trunk, reported that an elephant is like a very thick snake. A second beggar, who had put his arms around one of the elephant's legs, claimed that the elephant is like a column. "No! No!", shouted a third begger, who had felt an elephant's ear. "The elephant is like a flapping wing, only made of rough leather." "You are wrong,"

said a fourth, who had got hold of an elephant's tail. "An elephant is just like a rope."

In attempting to explain human social behavior we constantly run the risk of acting like the beggars in this ancient Persian story. Human social behavior being so varied and complex, it is tempting to simplify matters by isolating a piece of behavior and explaining it as a separate entity. The risk, of course, is to see the elephant as a rope or a pillar and miss not only the interconnection of the parts, but also the big picture.

On the other hand, the challenges of taking the whole picture into consideration seem awesome. After all, an elephant *is* very big, just as the behavior of persons in social contexts involves a vast range of influences. Many of these variables are included under the general title of culture.

The most striking thing about culture is that it is a complex phenomenon and difficult to define, as reflected by the hundreds of different definitions put forward in the literature (Keesing 1974; Shweder and LeVine 1984). In everyday usage, we often consider high culture as involving the opera, museums, and generally stylish living. The use of the term culture in this manner reflects a value preference, in favor of one style of life over others. In *Culture and Anarchy,* first published in 1869, the English social philosopher Matthew Arnold argues that, "...culture is, or ought to be, the study and pursuit of perfection..." (1960, 72). Arnold had in mind a certain kind of high culture associated with the classical roots of Western civilization. But culture, as defined by social scientists, does not involve value judgments about lifestyles.

We define culture broadly as *the human-made part of the environment,* following Herkovits (1948, 17). We adopt this definition because it presents culture, first, as a combination of both social and material products of humankind; second, as already being there when the individual arrives in the world; and, third, as more than all that is in the minds of individuals. From our perspective, material products such as roads, bridges, cooking pots, and military weapons are as much a part of a culture as are musical symphonies, poetry, and other social products. All such phenomena are made by humans, but—in turn—also help to "make" humans. In essence, humans have an interactive relationship with culture: we create and shape culture, and are in turn influenced by our own cultural products.

Because cultures vary in important ways across societies, the behavior of individuals also differs across societies. A clear implication is that those studying social behavior need to consider the role of culture. By incorporating culture in their research, social psychologists will be able to make more accurate generalizations about human behavior. For example, consider the issue of how much effort individuals put into a task when they are performing the task on their own, as opposed to when they are performing the task as a member of a group.

Research in North America (Latané, Williams, and Harkins 1979), as well as in some non-Western countries, such as India (Weiner, Pandy, and Latané 1981), shows that people exert more effort when working on a task individually than as part of a group. From one perspective, this seems a "natural" way to behave, because in a group setting the performance of each individual is less visible and, presumably, there is less motivation for individuals to exert themselves.

But it would be wrong for us to generalize and claim that people in all societies follow this pattern of behavior. For example, studies with Chinese respondents have found the *reverse* trend, showing that these subjects worked harder in groups than when on their own (Gabrenya, Latané, and Wang 1983; Gabrenya, Wang, and Latané 1985). Presumably, these Chinese subjects were more motivated when they worked in groups rather than on their own. Consequently, research in different societies allows us to make more accurate generalizations about the amount of effort people exert when working as individuals and as group members: not all humans "loaf" when put to work in a group.

For several important reasons, culture *has* a role in social behavior and should be part of social psychology, and we begin this chapter by clarifying these points. Next, we discuss why culture has been neglected by social psychologists. In the third part of the chapter, we discuss the ways in which culture is entering social psychology. Finally, we outline the cultural perspective that we see to be a means of making social psychology a universal science.

The Importance of Culture in Social Behavior

Our everyday experiences suggest that culture has a profound influence on behavior. Often, we first recognize this influence through the experience of travel abroad. The traveler in a foreign country has many opportunities to learn about some of the most immediately apparent aspects of a culture, such as local customs, food, clothing, speech, and behavior in public settings. For example, as a tourist in Saudi Arabia or some other Middle Eastern country, we would learn about the custom of bartering in the marketplace. Thus, when we spot something that we want to buy, we would not accept the first price the Saudi seller suggests, but would haggle over the cost and try to push it down. We may not become as effective in bargaining as the local inhabitants, but after even a few weeks we would find ourselves paying less, sometimes a great deal less, for the articles we buy.

Examples abound of how neglect of culturally appropriate behavior can have disastrous consequences. Some Westerners find themselves in jail in Muslim countries because they did not conform to local customs that prohibit alcoholic drinks and forbid men and women from showing intimacy toward each other in public places. Well-intentioned Western visitors to India can find themselves offending their hosts by following their own custom of eating all the food served them. By leaving some food on the plate, a guest in India indicates the generosity of the host, who had put so much food out that the guest could not possibly eat it all. Tourists to the Third World can find themselves surrounded by angry street beggars if they do not learn to give money in appropriate amounts to the appropriate beggars.

If we were to stay in a foreign country for a longer period, as diplomats and representatives of international corporations often do, we would begin to learn more fundamental characteristics of local cultures. For example, as a North American representative of an international company in Japan, we would gradually learn that Japanese society is more collectivistic than individualistic, relative to Western societies. A consequence of this is that in Japanese corporations individuals are evaluated on the basis of their contribution to the team, rather than how far they can push ahead of their colleagues. Edwin Reischauer (1988), a Harvard specialist on Japan, contrasts the situation of managers in the United States and Japan as follows:

> Japanese business executives are less concerned with quick profits to please stockholders than with long-term growth to increase the company's market share and win national and international prestige...Such attitudes contrast with American concentration on personal success in whatever company pays best and immediate profits to demonstrate personal effectiveness. (338)

But we need not travel to other societies to see the influence of culture on social behavior. Research among different groups *within* society also helps us to make more accurate generalizations—for example, about the social roles of different family members. This fact is illustrated in a dramatic way by Carol Stack (1974), in her studies of The Flats, the poorest section of a black community in the Midwestern city of Jackson Harbor. Stack found that among members of this community, household membership is often determined by such factors as the need to change domestic arrangements in order to remain eligible for welfare, rather than the emotional needs of individuals and their desire to live with particular others.

Within these conditions where steady employment is so difficult to find, Stack discovered that the culture of the low-income blacks she studied differs in important ways from that of middle-

and upper-income blacks and whites. Social roles such as that of father, for example, were different, so that a typical low-income black mother in Stack's sample generally regarded her children's father as a "friend of the family whom she can recruit for help, rather than as a father failing his parental duties....many fathers cannot be depended on as a steady source of help" (127). The middle-class father, on the other hand, is seen as having heavy parental obligations and a role almost as central as that of the mother in family life. By studying different groups within our own society, we are able to make more accurate generalizations about the behavior of people in different social roles, such as the "father" and "mother" roles.

Cultural differences across ethnic groups is particularly important in the United States, Canada, and other immigrant-receiving societies. North America has been described as a land of immigrants, and the cultural and linguistic diversity present in American and Canadian societies endorses this description. Historically, researchers have assumed that in the course of urbanization and industrialization, ethnic minorities would assimilate and disappear into the melting pot. In recent years, however, we have witnessed the rise of ethnicity. Researchers who have studied immigrant groups find that when they come to North America, there is a strong tendency for Greeks to want to retain their Greek identity, for Italians to desire to speak Italian, and for Arabs to want their children to be brought up according to traditional Arab values (see Lambert and Taylor 1990; Moghaddam and Taylor 1987; Moghaddam, Taylor, and Lalonde 1987, 1989). This motivation among immigrant groups to retain their traditional cultures is important because it suggests that cultural and linguistic diversity will continue in the United States and Canada.

In addition to the cultural diversity reflected by immigrant populations, various "ethnic power" movements, involving African Americans, Native people, and others, have involved an attempt to re-establish distinct cultural identities for ethnic minorities within a North American context. All of these developments have led to serious questioning of the "assimilationist assumption" (Glazer and

Moynihan 1970; Olzak 1983)—which proposes that minorities eventually assimilate into the mainstream—and to a growing recognition of the cultural diversity within North American society as well. Clearly, social psychologists in the United States need to consider cultural differences among ethnic groups in order to explain social behavior within their own society.

Although European countries are not traditionally viewed as being immigrant-receiving, cultural diversity also is present in Europe. This is in part because of the influx of "guest workers" to many European countries, such as the Turks in West Germany, but also because of the ties that European countries still have with their former colonies in Africa and Asia. These ties have led, for example, to the presence of several million South Asians in the United Kingdom and North Africans in France. The growing ethnic unrest in the former communist countries is also an example of the desire of groups to assert their ethnic and cultural independence and serves as a reminder of the strength of cultural diversity within European nations. Thus, even in Europe there is emphasis on cultural diversity and an increased awareness of society being composed of different ethnic and linguistic groups (Lambert, Moghaddam, et al. 1990).

Beyond the cultural differences associated with different ethnic and linguistic groups, there also exist major cultural divisions between social classes within each society. In the third-world context, such divisions are very apparent because of sharp distinctions between the modern and traditional sectors of societies. The modern sector is populated by an élite who also enjoy great power and status, and tend to have a Westernized lifestyle. The masses living in the traditional sector have less power, are poor, and are far more influenced by traditional tribal, religious, linguistic, and regional ties.

These divisions in third-world societies serve to remind us of the cultural divisions that also exist within industrial world societies. Such cultural divisions in North American society emerged in a cross-cultural study of child-rearing values, a study involving parents from eleven national groups and from a variety of socioeconomic backgrounds (Lambert 1987). The results of this study underscored cultural differences within each society.

> "One overriding outcome was the important influence of socioeconomic backgrounds on parents' values; social class turned out to have a much more powerful effect on parental values than ethnicity.... What this outcome means, in the present context, is that in order to make statements about national or cultural differences in values, the researcher must make provisions to control for social class whenever comparisons are made, since, in general, working-class parents from Italy, for example, are more similar to Japanese working-class parents in their child-rearing values than they are to Italian parents of middle-class socioeconomic standing, just as Japanese middle-class parents are more like Greek middle-class parents than they are like other Japanese from a different socioeconomic stratum. (Lambert 1987, 12).

Another important type of cultural difference found within societies exists in the business world. Researchers have studied the different cultures found within different corporations under the title of corporate culture (synonymous with organizational culture). This concept started to have a place of importance in the management literature of the late 1970s, although earlier references to it are found (Blake and Mouton 1964). During the 1950s and 1960s, researchers had discussed the different "climates" of various organizations, and there eventually emerged the idea that corporations, such as General Motors and Ford, have cultures that are in important ways different from each other (Deal and Kennedy 1982; Ott 1989; Pettigrew 1979; Schein 1985).

Researchers began studying the norms, values, rituals, symbols, and social interactions within organizations very much as if they were investigating social life in different tribes of people. Two well-known examples of this approach are Thomas Pettigrew's (1985) investigation of Imperial Chemical Industry (ICI), and Geert Hofstede's (1980) study of key social psychological variables among International Business Machines (IBM) employees around the world. While there are different approaches to studying corporate culture, the underlying assumption is that we should not assume all North American corporations, for example, to be the same, just because they are present in the same society. Within America, there are major cultural differences between corporations. For example, some corporations use "bottom-up" management techniques and look for initiative and direction from employees, while others are "top-directed," with initiatives and policies coming only from the top management.

Thus, culture has an important influence on social behavior and should have a central role in social psychology. Culture can help explain differences in social behavior across different societies. But there also exist important cross-cultural differences between groups within societies, such as those found across ethnic, social class, and corporate groups. Consequently, social psychologists also need to incorporate culture in their studies when they focus on behavior within societies.

Why Is Culture Not Considered in Social Psychology?

An ultimate goal of science is to discover universal principles. A principle is deemed universal when it explains a relationship between sets of variables in all conditions. For example, evolutionary theory as described by Charles Darwin in the *Origin of Species* (1859) predicts that individual differences within species will to a large extent determine the biological characteristics that are passed on to subsequent generations, as well as the ultimate survival of a species. This general principle is assumed to hold for all species, in all parts of the world. This does not mean, however, that variations in the environment do not play an important role in evolution. The characteristics that are more likely to survive from one generation to the next are those that help the organism survive and reproduce best in its particular environment.

In the same way, the science of social psychology attempts to discover universal principles of social behavior. Such principles aim to explain aspects of social behavior for all individuals in all social contexts. For example, a candidate for such a universal principle of social behavior might be the following: During interactions between two individuals (known as dyadic interactions), verbal communications are almost always initiated and terminated by the individual with higher status. In a meeting with the company president, for example, an employee would follow the cues given by the president to indicate when the meeting has formally begun and when it has ended. (This general trend seems to hold true across cultures, Brown 1966).

Social psychology so far has had limited success in establishing universal principles. This fact is usually explained by pointing out that, compared to biology, chemistry, and other more established disciplines, social psychology is a relatively young science. Although the first social psychology text written by a psychologist was published at the turn of the century (McDougall 1908), the main expansion of this discipline has taken place only in the last few decades.

Undoubtedly, the recentness of scientific social psychology has to some extent been responsible for the limited success of the discipline in establishing universal laws of social behavior. But another factor responsible for this situation is that social psychology has largely been shaped by researchers in only one country—the United States—and until very recently there were few members of minority groups among professional social psychologists or the subjects they studied. Thus, social psychology is largely monocultural in that both the researchers attracted to the discipline and the subjects it has studied share a single culture. Yehuda Amir and Irit Sharon (1987), two Israeli psychologists, have claimed that, "For all intents and purposes, social psychology is the study of second-year American psychology students" (385). Historically, both researchers and subjects in social psychological studies have shared a lifestyle and value system that differs not only from that of most other people in North America, such as ethnic minorities and women, but also the vast majority of people in the rest of the world.

Of course, if universal principles can be generated, they can be by anyone, regardless of race, gender, or social class. But such success can only come about if ethnocentrism is avoided. That is, if researchers can generate and address research questions without being limited by the characteristics, such as values and perceptions, of their own culture. Unfortunately, ethnocentrism, involving a belief in the superiority of one's own cultural group, has influenced research in social psychology so that even some of the most established findings in social psychology do not stand up to the test when assessed in cultures outside North America. Three examples given below clarify this point, although many additional examples are discussed throughout the chapters of this text.

Example 1: Under the title "Are social-psychological laws cross-culturally valid?", Amir and Sharon (1987) report the findings of a research program that essentially set out to replicate studies representative of mainstream social psychology in another cultural context. Six studies were selected from major social psychological journals, and replicated with two Israeli samples, one similar and the other different from samples in the original study. The replication studies did not confirm the main findings of the original studies. For example, one study focused on the effectiveness of tactics used by people to get others to like or dislike them. American students used in the original study proved to be fairly effective at getting others to like them, whereas the replication studies were relatively unsuccessful. This failure to reproduce the findings is even more surprising because of the inclusion of students in the replications. These students presumably shared many similarities with the English and North American students used in the original studies. For example, they were similar in terms of age, socioeconomic status, and educational experience.

Example 2: Research in the United States demonstrates that, at least under some conditions, norms of reciprocity ("give and take") influence behavior in such a way that the more person P receives from person O, the more he or she will want to give in return (Pruitt 1968). Studies show that reciprocity behavior can be induced by a variety of experimental procedures, such as providing individuals with unreasonably high outcomes for performing a given task. In North America, overpaid subjects have been found to do more or better work than subjects who are paid equitably (Walster, Walster, and Berscheid 1978), but this reaction was not that of Dutch (Wilke and Steur 1972) or Italian (Gergen, Morse, and Bode 1974) subjects. Another strategy for inducing reciprocity behavior was used by Feldman (1968), in a study where cashiers in pastry shops in Athens, Boston, and Paris, were overpaid for purchases made by "customers" (collaborating with the experimenter). Whereas 82 percent of the cashiers in Boston refunded the overpayment, only 46 percent of those in Paris and 49 percent in Athens did so. In comparing how Austrian and American subjects distribute rewards to individuals performing tasks, Mikula (1974) found that Americans do seem to strive for equity between input and outcome, but the main emphasis of the Austrians was on equity of one person's outcomes with another.

Example 3: One of the most influential social psychological theories to emerge from research in the United States is Leon Festinger's (1957) theory of cognitive dissonance. This theory proposes that individuals will feel tension ("dissonance") when they become aware that two of their thoughts or beliefs ("cognitions") are inconsistent. Hundreds of studies carried out in Western societies support Festinger's prediction that people adjust their thinking in order to reduce this tension (e.g., Kahle and Beatty 1987). But there is also evidence that cognitive dissonance theory does not explain behavior well in some non-Western societies, such as Japan (Iwao 1988). According to Gui-Young Hong (1992), in Japan how well a person handles a supposed "inconsistency" is considered a sign of maturity and broad-mindedness. The Japanese are socialized to accept the supposed inconsistency, rather than to try to resolve it in the way Festinger predicted. These studies demonstrate the need to take into account cultural differences when making generalizations from studies carried out in the United States.

Thus, a challenge confronting contemporary social psychology is to more fully address those questions that it *has* raised. Ethnocentrism has sometimes crept into research, so that questions have been addressed through the limited perspective of only one culture. Consequently, the generalizations that can be made on the basis of research findings have limited accuracy. As soon as we enter cultural contexts outside mainstream North America, many such generalizations become questionable.

But there is also the additional challenge that social psychology needs to be more expansive in the questions it does raise. Particularly with respect to relations between large social groups, social psychology needs to address many additional questions that are important from the perspective of minority groups and cultures outside the United States. This situation will improve as U.S. social psychologists become more open to the influence of researchers in other parts of the world. So far, researchers in the United States have not taken sufficient interest in social psychology in other parts of the world (Lewicki 1982; Moghaddam 1987). However, there are signs that that situation may be changing.

How Culture Is Being Introduced into Social Psychology

Changes at two levels, within U.S. society and internationally, are gradually leading researchers to reassess the role of culture in social psychology.

Social Psychology Within the United States

Culture is being introduced into social psychology as students and teachers of social psychology, as well as subjects in social psychological research, begin to come from more diverse backgrounds. As a result, the basic questions addressed in social psychology are beginning to change. The widely varying life-conditions of various social groups, such as ethnic minorities, low-income groups, gays, and women, often lead them to approach issues from a new perspective and to ask alternative questions.

The treatment of gender in social psychology illustrates this point. During the early years of the discipline, there were few female students in universities and even fewer female teachers of social psychology. One of the consequences was that the possibility of gender differences in social behavior was not a major focus for research. In many studies, the sex of the subjects was not even reported. It was either assumed that all the subjects were male, or that whatever results were achieved with male subjects would hold true for female subjects. Gradually, as the number of female social psychology students increased in the post Second-World-War period, the literature on sex differences began to grow. Female students began to question themselves and their teachers as to whether certain research findings would hold true for a female population. For example, in experiments on conformity, women proved to be obedient to authority in the same way as men (Milgram 1974). In contrast, research on empathy showed that women are more likely than men to feel what another person feels (Eisenberg and Lennon 1983). As a consequence, there has emerged a greater focus on gender differences in research (Doyle and Paludi 1991).

More recently, the women's movement has led to a fundamental re-evaluation of how we conceptualize and measure gender. Traditionally, an individual was assumed to be either masculine or feminine. Researchers typically would measure masculinity and femininity by asking respondents to choose between these two poles. Feminist researchers such as Sandra Bem (1974 1984), however, argued that people combine both masculine and feminine qualities to different degrees, and that androgynous individuals, those combining both feminine and masculine traits, can be high on both masculinity and femininity. Once freed from traditional sex roles, individuals can be assertive and tough one minute and warm and caring the next. A consequence of the concept of androgyny was that in measuring masculinity and femininity, researchers began to ask questions in such a way as to allow for the possibility that an individual might be high on both traits. As with gender, the interest of culture in social psychology and the growth of social psychology outside the United States is leading to new perspectives and raising important questions.

Social Psychology in the International Context

> Psychologists from all over the world, and particularly from Western Europe, flock to the United States in much the same way, and for essentially the same reasons, as painters flocked to Italy in the seventeenth century and to France in the early twentieth century....In fact, a Western European psychologist is not held to have completed his studies or to have won the right to speak authoritatively on psychological matters until he has spent some time at an American university. (Berlyne 1968, 477)

This evaluation made a quarter of a century ago remains, to a large extent, true today. The United States is the world center of psychology, and of social psychology in particular. From the beginning, social psychology was a U.S.-based enterprise and the social psychology being taught in classrooms around the world is heavily influenced by U.S. models of social behavior. Some of these models may have little relevance or appeal in a different cultural context.

A historic example of such a model is John Thibaut and Harold Kelley's (1959) analysis of social relations as transactions. According to these researchers, transactions are based on an individual's assessments of how likely other people are to bring him or her the highest satisfaction, in terms of a maximum of rewards and a minimum of penalties. But this kind of rational, market-based model of social relations is shaped by the values of middle-class U.S. culture, and often it is only when people from other backgrounds become familiar with middle-class U.S. culture that such models make sense to them. Serge Moscovici, a leading French social psychologist since the 1970s, has noted that he could not comprehend Thibaut and Kelley's model until he traveled to the United States and came to appreciate its background. Moscovici (1972) concluded that "...in Europe, we must turn towards our own reality, towards our own maxims from which we must derive our own 'scientific' consequences" (19).

A distinct European social psychology became a reality in part because the human expertise and research facilities needed for a non-U.S. social psychology to develop have become available in Europe. Particularly since the late 1960s, European social psychology has developed characteristics different from U.S. social psychology. Through the influence of social psychologists such as Henri Tajfel (1984) at Bristol University, England, Rom Harré (1984, 1985, 1990) at Oxford University, England, Serge Moscovici (1985) at the École des Hautes Études en Sciences Sociales, France, and Willem Doise (1978) of Geneva University, Switzerland, European social psychology has become more *social* than U.S. social psychology. By this is meant that there has been in European social psychology a greater focus on larger societal issues, such as intergroup relations, unemployment, and ideology. An important lesson from this research is that we can achieve a better explanation of social behavior when we study individuals during interactions with others and in relation to group processes, rather than in isolation.

Intergroup relations, in particular, has become a major focus of social psychological research in Europe. Henri Tajfel, the father of European social psychology, and his students have made intergroup relations the main topic of their studies and European social psychology texts devote major chapters to this topic (Hewstone et al. 1988; Tajfel and Fraser 1978). In contrast, intergroup relations remains a neglected topic in U.S. social psychology and very few U.S. texts devote chapters to this topic. An example of the interesting research coming out of this European focus is studies on how minority groups can influence majority groups (Moscovici 1985). We discuss this European research in Chapter 5.

Just as European social psychology has begun to develop a distinct character, there are promising signs of a distinct social psychology in the Third World. Although third-world social psychologists suffer from a lack of resources (Adair 1989; Sinha and Holtzman 1984), some progress is being made toward developing a social psychology that meets the genuine needs of third-world societies (Moghaddam 1990), particularly in India (Misra 1990; Sinha 1986). Western researchers may in turn learn from the social psychological research being conducted in the Third World. For example, Western researchers can learn valuable lessons from poverty research in India. An unexpected discovery made by Indian researchers is that changing only one aspect of the social situation of the poor can lead to undesirable consequences. Durganand Sinha (1974), a leading Indian psychologist, has identified some counter-productive consequences in the educational context, where materially disadvantaged students suffer in performance relative to advantaged children when they are transferred to "better" schools. Research on the experiences of disadvantaged children in Indian schools may help us understand more fully the complexities of desegregation in North American schools.

Another area in which non-Western psychological research may have valuable lessons for Western psychology is leader- ship behavior. Research in the West has focused on leadership types classified according to dichotomies such as: progressive/ conservative, democrative/autocratic, and nondirective/directive. Non-Western researchers have described these labels as being derived from Western values, and not necessarily appropriate for non-Western societies. For example, inherent in this research is the assumption that the best leader is "progressive, democratic, non-directive," as these terms are defined in the West. But this assumption is not necessarily appropriate in another culture. Accordingly, alternative approaches to studying leadership have been developed. For example, Indian researchers have worked on a model of a "nurturant task leader" (J. B. P. Sinha 1980), but the most well-developed leadership model that has evolved outside the West is probably that of Jyuji Misumi (1985), a Japanese researcher.

Misumi's "Performance-Maintenance" (PM) model centers around the idea of basic group functions. The first, P, is the function of contributing toward a group's problem solving; the second, M, is the function of preserving the group. A promising feature of Misumi's research is that it shows new approaches through which work productivity can be improved by appropriate leadership training. But Misumi acknowledges that his findings may be specific to Japanese culture, so that a "...next step in the PM leadership research program will be to determine whether or not its results can be applied to non-Japanese cultures" (332). Despite these possible limitations, research by Misumi and other non-Western psychologists can provide valuable lessons for Western psychologists.

Culture and Social Psychology: Toward a Solution

By adopting a cross-cultural perspective, social psychologists will be better able to explain human social behavior. Adopting a cross-cultural perspective requires, first, that culture be included as an integral part of social psychological theories; second, that cultural variables be included in empirical studies (Jahoda 1980). In the following discussion, we shall review psychological differentiation theory to illustrate how the incorporation of culture in theory and empirical studies can enrich our understanding of social behavior.

According to the theory of psychological differentiation, psychological development involves a progression from undifferentiated to increasingly differentiated functioning (Witkin, Lewis et al. 1954; Witkin, Dyk et al. 1962). In this context, "differentiation" means, first, distinguishing between two or more phenomena; second, relating and integrating these distinguished phenomena.

There are two aspects to this progression—internal and external. Psychological processes such as feeling, perceiving, and thinking, are differentiated internally. For example, during the course of development, the individual learns to differentiate between various feelings, such as anger and shame. Externally, there is a clearer distinction between the self and nonself elements in the environment. For example, particularly in Western cultures, individuals learn to make sharp distinctions between events caused by factors "inside" themselves, as opposed to those caused by external factors. Thus, relative to the infant, the adult personality is a more complex structure, composed of differentiated, integrated elements.

Social differentiation theory proposes that differentiation is universal, in that all humans pass from a less to a more differentiated state during their development. However, the theory also focuses on *diversity* in social differentiation among different people, and sees culture as a major source of this diversity. In particular, the theory proposes that the culture influences differentiation through socialization practices, basically "how" children are "brought up." Generally speaking, more permissive socialization practices lead to greater differentiation, and stricter ones to less differentiation. This proposition has been particularly well studied through research on field dependence/independence.

The terms "field dependence" and "field independence" represent a continuum on which individuals can be placed, to indicate how dependent or independent on cues in the environment ("field") their perceptions are. Two experimental methods used to assess field dependence/independence are the Rod and Frame Test (RFT), and the Embedded Figures Test (EFT). In the RFT, respondents must adjust a tilted rod to a position that seems to them to be vertical. This rod is enclosed in a frame that is inclined by 28 degrees. "Field-independent" respondents are those who are more accurate in adjusting the rod; "field-dependent" respondents are distracted by the surrounding frame, so that they do this task less well. In the EFT, the task is to locate and recognize a simple figure contained in a relatively complex one. On this task, field-independent respondents are more successful at extracting a part of the figure from the whole.

John Berry (1976) reasoned that the ecocultural conditions of groups with different economic support systems, such as agriculturalists and hunters, should lead to differences in field dependence/independence. For example, hunters will depend to a greater degree than agriculturalists on their differentiating and reconstructing skills, so that they can pick out the relevant signs, tracks, odors, and sounds, from the surroundings. In order to survive, hunters must be able to sharply distinguish between different features of the environment, including the paths that lead them back to home. Agriculturalists, in contrast, have less need to wander into unfamiliar territory and, consequently, would be less dependent on powers of differentiation. Consequently, Berry predicted, and experimentally confirmed in a seventeen-culture study, greater field independence among hunters and higher dependence among agriculturalists.

Other research has focused on the socialization processes leading to differences on field dependence/independence among groups with different ecocultural conditions (Witkin and Berry 1975). For example, the mothers of field-dependent children tend to limit their childrens' outdoor activities and to encourage conformity and dependence. Mothers of field-independent children, in contrast, encourage independence and autonomous behavior.

In addition to a focus on cultural diversity across societies, psychological differentiation theory has led to a concern for cultural diversity *within* societies. For example, certain types of societies, those characterized by "high food accumulation" where large animals are domesticated—for example, the Zulu in South Africa and the Maori in New Zealand—show significant sex differences in psychological differentiation. In these societies, females tend to be more field dependent and males more field independent (Van Leeuwen 1978). This may be because in these agricultural societies a greater emphasis is placed on obedience and responsibility in the socialization of females, whose duties are in or very close to the home.

Thus, on the one hand, empirical research on field dependence/independence has endorsed the proposition that the developmental process from less to more differentiation is universal. On the other hand, this research has identified associations between aspects of culture, such as socialization practices, and behavioral differences. This research represents an example of a cross-cultural perspective, which promises to truly establish social psychology as a science of *human* behavior. The challenge we take up in this text is to discuss important aspects of social behavior from a cross-cultural perspective.

Replication can be of value (e.g., Amir and Sharon 1988), but if social psychologists are not selective in what they replicate, this process could lead to frustration among students and researchers, and stagnation in the field. Instead, we have proposed that students of social psychology adopt a more far-reaching cross-cultural perspective, one involving a general sensitivity to the role of culture in social behavior.

Plan of this Book

The six chapters in this book all share the overarching theme of culture and behavior. In each chapter, a different topic is discussed with the purpose of showing how a consideration for culture can enrich our understanding of social behavior. We begin with a discussion of research methods in Chapter 2. Students of social behavior have available to them a wide array of powerful research methods, from tightly controlled laboratory procedures to field methods involving less control of the variables on the part of researchers. A common feature of all such research methods is that culture plays a central part in them, in the sense that their effectiveness depends in large part on how people interpret and evaluate them. For example, the laboratory experiment, by far the most widely used research method, can best work in a context where people share Western understandings of "science," "research," "subject," "data," and the like. In essence, research methods both are cultural products and lead to results that need to be interpreted in cultural context.

The general topic of cognitive social psychology is discussed in Chapter 3, with a more specific focus on attitudes, attributions, and stereotypes. Cross-cultural differences in attitudes, attributions, and stereotypes mean that when measuring these phenomena we need to consider cultural factors. For example, in North America the prevailing social norm is for people not to frankly express negative attitudes toward other groups—even racists tend to comply with these prevailing norms and shy away from publicly expressing racist attitudes. In contrast, people in India will often express their negative attitudes toward other groups very frankly.

Social influence, the most controversial topic in social psychology, is the subject of Chapter 4. Perhaps the main reason why studies on social influence are so controversial is that they demonstrate limitations on individual freedom. For example, they show that "normal" persons can be influenced by an authority figure to inflict severe pain on others. Such findings are particularly problematic from the perspective of Western cultures, which give a central role to "individual responsibility" and "self-help." If people can be influenced by others to such high degrees as suggested by the research evidence, to what extent are we justified in holding individuals responsible for their actions? This dilemma is less problematic in cultures where collective responsibility and collective effort are given primary importance.

Social relations is the topic of the fifth chapter. A cross-cultural approach to how we treat others and feel about them proves to be particularly effective in highlighting differences in behavior between people in individualistic and collectivistic societies. For example, by selecting to study topics such as romantic couples or first-time acquaintances, rather than kinship and community, researchers have shown a cultural bias toward topics that are normative for Western rather than for more traditional societies. Western societies are more individualistic, and social relations in these societies involve mobile and "free" individuals interacting with one another. The unit of concern in such societies is the individual person. In contrast, the unit of concern in traditional societies is the collective whole. Individual mobility is minimal, and kin and community play a far greater role in social relations between people. Societies high in individualism involve sharp boundaries around the self and between individuals; whereas those high in collectivism have far more fuzzy boundaries around the self and between individuals.

Finally, in the sixth chapter we discuss how a cross-cultural approach to social behavior can help social scientists in applied settings. Included in Chapter 6 are considerations of contact between cultural groups in business and other contexts, re-entry to a culture after a period of living abroad, and multiculturalism. These topics are gaining in importance at the global level, in part because the "global village" is now becoming a reality. Many individuals and groups, multinational corporations among them, have discovered that to make progress in today's world, it is necessary to take cultural factors into consideration.

2

Research Methods in Cultural Context

In all domains of science, researchers have to follow systematic procedures in order to gather data. The term "research methods" is used to refer to these procedures. A great variety of research methods are available to social psychologists (Aronson, Brewer and Carlsmith 1985; Kidder and Judd 1986; King and Ziegler 1975). These methods include the *laboratory experiment, field experiment, natural experiment, survey, controlled observation,* and *participant observation.* The order in which we have listed these methods corresponds to the degree of control that is exerted by the researcher, descending from a high degree of control (laboratory experiment) to a low degree (participant observation). Interestingly, this order also corresponds to the popularity of each method in social psychology—probably because research methods that allow a higher degree of control are seen as more scientific. For this reason, social psychologists have adopted these methods as part of their strategy to legitimize their work as scientific.

Although the range of research methods is fairly wide, surveys of the leading journals reveal that in practice the majority of social psychological research is carried out in the laboratory (Christie 1965; Fried et al. 1973; Higbee and Wells 1972; Sears 1986). In fact, while criticisms of the laboratory method were probably most intense during the late 1960s and the 1970s, the percentage of laboratory studies published in the *Journal of Personality and Social Psychology* actually increased from 72.0 percent in 1969 to 77.1 percent in 1979 (Adair et al. 1985). Thus, the commitment of social psychologists to the laboratory method, as reflected by at least one prestigious journal is apparently on the increase. More recent reviews confirm the central place of laboratory procedures in social psychology (Aronson, Brewer et al. 1985; Aronson, Ellsworth et al. 1990).

In a systematic survey of the samples used in social psychological research, David Sears (1986) has shown that since the 1960s over 80 percent of social psychological studies have relied exclusively on college students tested in the laboratory context. Furthermore, the vast majority of these students have been recruited from undergraduate classes in psychology. Sears argues convincingly that this "narrow data base" has biased social psychology's view of human nature. According to this view, for example, people readily change their attitudes and are easily influenced socially. These characteristics seem to be more true for 18- to 22-year-olds, who are still in a stage of identity development in Western cultures, than it is for older people, whose attitudes and values have become more stable (see Sears 1986, 423).

In this chapter we first review the main research methods in order to clarify the role of cultural context in classic studies using each method. Second, we shall focus on how a cross-cultural perspective can enrich topical methods of research and improve our understanding of social behavior in important ways.

Cross-cultural psychologists study behavior across different cultures. However, they are keenly aware that culture is a complex and multifaceted phenomenon (Triandis and Berry 1980). The complexity of culture means that when we find differences in behavior across cultures, it is not easy to identify their source. For example, if we find that North Americans are more competitive than South Asians, to what should we attribute this difference? Biological factors? Economic factors? Family structure? Early socialization? This dilemma confronts cross-cultural psychologists in an obvious way, because they deal with the large variable, "culture." But it also confronts social psychologists researching within their own societies, dealing with large variables such as sex, ethnicity, and social class.

At the simplest level, cross-cultural methodology involves incorporating respondents from more than one culture in a study (Triandias and Berry 1980). For example, by including samples of respondents from the United States and from Germany, we can address the question, "How obedient are people in the United States as compared to Germans?" At a more complex level, cross-cultural research involves incorporating "stimulus equivalents"— that is, stimuli that exist in different cultures and are different from each other on the surface, but serve the same functions. For example, the scientist in a white lab coat is a symbol of authority in Western cultures, just as the village chief or the army officer is the symbol of authority in some traditional societies. The vast majority of cross-cultural studies have simply involved comparisons across samples from different cultures, and have neglected the more complex task of incorporating "stimulus equivalents."

The Laboratory Experiment as Drama

The research methods available to social psychologists have traditionally been differentiated in terms of the amount of control that the researcher can exert when using each method. However, another way of reviewing social psychological research methods is to consider the level of "stage management" that has to go on when employing each method. From this perspective, the experimenter can be viewed as a dramatist, who has to prepare the script, set the stage, and supervise the rehearsals until the players can deliver a polished performance (Moghaddam and Harré 1992). One of the benefits of considering the role of the experimenter as dramatist is that the cultural context of the study is better revealed. This is particularly true for the laboratory experiment.

Like all dramas, laboratory experiments are based on scripts. The script for an experiment specifies the context, as well as the dialogue. But there is a gap in this script, and it is this gap that the subject is asked to fill. The other players on the set very often have a prescribed script. They are "collaborators" or "stooges" of the experimenter, and they rehearse their parts so that they will be able to convince the subjects of the authenticity of the plot.

Setting the Stage

The laboratory in social psychology consists of a separated space in which variables can be controlled. This space may be a simple room or a specially designed setting with one-way mirrors, dividing screens, computers, video and sound-recording equipment, and other facilities to study behavior. But whether the laboratory environment is simple or sophisticated, the first task of the experimenter is to set the stage for the experiment in a convincing manner. While researchers have more control over variables in the laboratory setting, they also have to do more "stage managing" in this setting. The experimenter tries to do this by creating a compelling "cover story." The success of an experiment depends largely on the credibility of this cover story; an experiment with a weak cover story is likely to fail. However, a story that has meaning and acts as a "good cover" in the context of one culture may not be so effective in the context of another.

Although the laboratory experiment is seen as the most objective and "scientific" method in social psychology, it needs artistic skills to create a good cover story and to act it out convincingly. For example, let us consider Stanley Milgram's (1974) research on obedience to authority, one of the best-known series of experiments in the history of social psychology. The cover story for these experiments was simple but convincing in the United States, where the study was originally carried out: subjects were told that they were taking part in a study investigating the effect of punishment on learning.

However, this would not be an effective cover story in some traditional cultures, where psychological research as we know it in the West does not exist. For example, in a traditional Indian village, the explanation that "this is an experiment about the effect of punishment on learning" would probably be answered by such questions as, "What is an experiment?", and "You say you are a researcher, what do you do?" This does not mean that research on obedience to authority could not be carried out in a traditional Indian village. However, what it does suggest is that cultural symbols and cover stories appropriate to the traditional Indian village culture would have to be introduced.

In the Milgram experiment, the naive subject was introduced to another person, supposedly also a subject but in reality a confederate of the experimenter. Then the two subjects drew lots to see who would act as the learner and who would be the teacher. In fact, the real subject was always assigned the role of teacher. The subject and confederate learner were taken to adjoining rooms, in one of which the learner was strapped to a chair with an electrode on his or her wrist. The real subject was positioned in the next room, behind a panel of switches that ostensibly could be used to administer electric shocks to the learner. The switches were set at 15-volt intervals up to 450 volts, with labels from "slight shock" (15–60 volts), through to "Danger: severe shock" (375–420 volts) and finally "XX" (435–460 volts). The subject was given a sample shock of 45 volts, so that he or she would know what the shocks were like.

The procedure was simple: the subject read out pairs of words, then read out the first word in each pair followed by four possible associates for the "learner" to choose from. The subject was to punish each incorrect response the "learner" made by administering an electric shock, increasing the level of shock after each trial. In fact, the confederate "learner" received no shocks but acted "as if" experiencing varying degrees of pain.

Almost two-thirds of the subjects obeyed the instructions of the experimenter and increased the voltage level up to the danger zone. Subjects often did show signs of uncertainty and even discomfort about giving the "learner" a 300-volt shock while the poor learner was pounding on the wall and screaming "Get me out of here!"; but most respondents went ahead and gave the shock anyway! The reassurance that subjects received from the authority figure in the white lab coat seemed to be enough to cast aside their doubts.

Controlling the Variables on the Set

The term "control" refers to the influence that experimenters have on the variables present in a situation. It is useful to think of these variables as being of three kinds. The first of these are independent variables, and it is the effect of these that experimenters want to understand. Examples of independent variables used by Milgram were proximity and having "subjects" (actually, confederates of the experimenter) present who refused to administer electric shocks to the learner. Milgram found that having subjects stand close to the confederate learner, and the presence of other confederate subjects who refused to administer shocks, decreased the willingness of actual subjects to administer shocks.

The second kind of variables are the dependent variables; experimenters monitor changes in these variables in order to identify the effect of changes in the independent variables. Thus, the researcher may measure the level of shock that a subject gives the learner in the Milgram experiment, and use this as an indicator of aggression shown by the subject.

The third kind of variables are "nuisance" variables; we can liken these to the "noise" that has to be eliminated so that we can identify the relationship between the independent and dependent variables more clearly. An example of a nuisance variable that needed to be controlled in the Milgram study is the personality profile of the subject sample. This is because the level of shock administered by the subjects could have been due to high levels of psychopathology among the subjects selected. Thus, in order to exclude the influence of this nuisance variable, Milgram screened the subjects first and only selected individuals who had normal personality profiles.

A Cross-Cultural Look at the Laboratory Experiment

The first point to be made is that culture *is* involved in the laboratory context. After clarifying this point, we further discuss the issue of stimulus equivalence using the example of the Milgram study.

The Culture of the Laboratory Setting: Imagine that you are asked to act as a subject in a laboratory experiment. The first thing you are likely to do is start wondering about what the experimenter is "really" up to. When you enter the laboratory, you do not walk into a cultural vacuum. On the contrary, you enter the laboratory with a host of ideas and expectations about what a laboratory experiment is, and about the role and character of psychologists and psychological research, among other things. Second, the experimenters will act out their parts in order to "set the stage" for the experiment, and they will attempt to get you, the subject, to see the experimental situation the way they themselves want it to be seen for the purposes of the experiment. Thus, the experimenters will carefully select a set of cues that they believe will lead you to see the situation the way it is "meant to be seen" in order for the experiment to work.

An essential part of the culture in the laboratory context are the roles of the subject and the experimenter. These roles are based on a number of shared understandings about the nature of science and of research, and about what researchers and human subjects are supposed to do. We should keep in mind that these shared understandings are part of a larger culture that has evolved in industrial societies. For example, as stated earlier, the scientist in a white lab coat is a symbol of authority in the Western societies. This is why Milgram was able to use this symbol so effectively in his research.

A Cross-Cultural Look at the Milgram Study: Milgram found that about 65 percent of both student and nonstudent samples in the United States were fully obedient. Replications of the Milgram study in Italy (Ancona and Pareyson 1968), Germany (Mantell 1971), Australia (Kilham and Mann 1974), and Jordan (Shanab and Yahya 1977) have revealed considerable cross-cultural variation, from 85 percent obedience registered by German respondents to 40 percent registered by Australian respondents. An adaptation of the Milgram procedures also revealed a high level (90 percent) of obedience among Dutch respondents under certain conditions (Meeus and Raajmakers 1986). Cross-cultural differences in obedience have also been found among children. For example, children sampled from the Kikuyu of East Africa proved to be more obedient than children in the United States (Munroe et al. 1981). Thus, comparisons of samples from different cultures reveal differences in obedience.

But a cross-cultural approach leads us to look beyond simple replications of studies. The Milgram obedience study could only be replicated using the same stimuli if respondents share the Western views about "authority figures," "science," "research," among other things. By looking beyond the realm of influence of western culture and imagining how we would conduct the Milgram study in a society that has other symbols of authority, we achieve a clearer understanding of the role of science and the scientist in our own society. In the West, the scientist has come to represent authority, just as the army officer or tribal chief represents authority in other societies.

Science is sometimes described as the "new religion" in Western societies, and it often has the authority and influence that major religions have in traditional cultures. But Western science and Western-trained scientists are not always respected in other cultures. For example, one of us was present during the "cultural revolution" in post-revolution Iran. During this period, much like the cultural revolution in China during the late 1960s, the universities were closed and Western-trained scientists became the target of suspicion and persecution. In this context, the scientist in the white lab coat would have made a pathetic authority figure, but the mullah would have made a very powerful one. Clearly, the high status and role that the scientist has in Western societies is not universal.

Viewed in this way, the Milgram study says more about the responsibilities, or perhaps "irresponsibilities", that the scientist has in modern society than about anything else. Using the authority of their role, scientists have the ability to influence people in important ways, and in many domains they *are* exerting this influence, both directly and indirectly.

In summary, the laboratory method allows for a precise manipulation of the variables and a measurement of changes in dependent variables as a result of changes in independent variables. Because of this control, the laboratory method is said to have high internal validity. In the laboratory experiment, we can be relatively sure that the measures are measuring what they are supposed to measure. However, we can be less sure that the results have high external validity, that is, that the measures used in the laboratory are measuring phenomena that exist outside the laboratory. Thus, we can be less sure about how valid it is to generalize from laboratory results to the outside world. The laboratory method can be used effectively to study the same processes in different cultures, but an important prerequisite for this study is the adoption of appropriate stimulus equivalents. Thus, to use the Milgram example, different symbols of authority might be selected for research in different cultural settings.

Field Research

Only a small minority of research studies in social psychology are currently carried out in the field (Sears 1986). For example, of all the research reported in the *Journal of Personality and Social*

Psychology, about 13 percent are field studies (Adair et al. 1985). There are several reasons for this, not the least important being that researchers are not able to control and manipulate variables as effectively in the field setting as they can in the laboratory context. But another reason is that field research requires a great deal more funding and time.

In a field study, there is some manipulation and "stage setting" by the experimenter. The field study takes place in a "naturalistic" context, involving social situations in everyday life, which gives it the advantage of greater realism over the laboratory experiment. A classic example of a field study is Muzafer Sherif's (1966) studies on conflict and cooperation among social groups, conducted in collaboration with his wife Carolyn Sherif and carried out in a boys' summer camp. These studies captured the imagination of many students, perhaps because the studies were so successful at manipulating variables in a naturalistic setting with which people could identify.

The achievement of Sherif lies in that he reproduced in a realistic manner some fundamental processes of group competition and cooperation. The findings of his research, and particularly the concept of superordinate goals, have been used to discuss conflict resolution at a variety of levels, from those of management-labor relations to those of the Superpowers. There were three stages to Sherif's study. In stage one, the boys were given sets of tasks to carry out in groups, and interactions between group members led to the development of group identity, groups norms, and a hierarchy of group members. At this stage, members of each group were unaware of the presence of the other group. When they were made aware that another group of boys was present nearby, competitive feelings developed immediately.

This awareness marked the start of the second stage of the study, the stage of intergroup competition. During this stage, the two groups engaged in a series of games and activities, in the course of which rivalry between them increased sharply. Hostilities intensified to the level of violence, and more aggressive leaders emerged in both groups. Ethnocentrism and the "we are better than they are" attitude was strengthened. Members of each group called the other group "stinkers," "cheats," and "sneaks," and the banners and flags of the other group were seized and burned.

The third stage of intergroup cooperation began with the introduction of "superordinate goals" by the experimenters. These are goals that each group wants to achieve, but cannot do so without the cooperation of the other group. For example, in one situation the cooperation of boys from both groups was needed in order to help start a truck that was to bring them food. If anything would get a bunch of growing boys working together, it was food! Superordinate goals helped to break down hostilities by providing a functional basis for the cooperation of all the boys. The leadership structure changed again, with the more aggressive leaders now being less prominent. This reminds us of the cooperation that is achieved between otherwise competing powers when a major crisis confronts the international community. For example, following earthquakes in Armenia (then part of the Soviet Union) in December 1988, food, clothing, and medical supplies were rushed to Armenia from many countries of the world, including the United States.

A Cross-Cultural Look at the Field Study

Because field studies are conducted in contexts that are culturally richer than laboratory studies, we should be even more attentive to cultural factors when interpreting their results. First, there is the question of the meaning of the context itself. Just as the psychology laboratory is a product of industrial societies, and has a special meaning for the people of these societies that is often not shared by people from other societies, so too the context of a field study frequently has a meaning unique to a certain society. For example, "boys' summer camps" play a certain role in North American culture that is not found in other cultures. Second, there is the question of the appropriateness of different types of behavior in certain settings. For example, the boys in Sherif's studies interpreted the situation as one in which competition or cooperation for scarce resources would be appropriate. Whether the boys competed or cooperated with the other group depended directly on which strategy best served their material interests. Such interpretations have a cultural basis.

An attempt to replicate Sherif's studies failed in the context of a summer camp in Lebanon (Diab 1970). The respondents in this study were 11-year-old boys, selected to be as comparable as possible to Sherif's 1966 sample. The same stages of group formation and intergroup competition were followed in the Diab replication, but there was an unexpected ending to the study. It proved impossible for the experimenters to get the two groups to cooperate, in part because of the intense resentment and frustration felt by the group that had lost in the main intergroup competitions. The study had to be abandoned. This failure to replicate Sherif's results underlines the importance of the cultural context of such studies.

Among the factors that had an important influence on Sherif's findings were competitiveness versus cooperation, and individualism versus collectivism. North American culture strongly endorses competitiveness, as well as individualism (Sampson 1977; Taylor and Moghaddam 1987). Cross-cultural studies among children similar in age to Sherif's respondents, show competitiveness to be particularly high among Westerners generally, and among North Americans in particular (Seymour 1981). For example, Anglo-American children compete more than do either Mexican or Mexican-American children (Madsen and Shapira 1970), and more than children in Kenya (Munroe and Munroe 1977); Canadian children compete more than do Native American children (Miller 1973); white Australian children compete more than do aboriginal children (Sommerlad and Bellingham 1972).

But these studies also reveal differences between children from urban and rural areas *within* the same societies. For example, rural Maori children were found to be less competitive than urban Maori children (Thomas 1975); and kibbutz children (who had grown up together in small rural communities) proved to be less competitive than urban Israeli children (Shapira and Madsen 1969, 1974). This suggests that competitiveness is nurtured in the urban environment, and that we also need to keep in mind differences in behavior across urban/rural contexts within societies.

With respect to differences across societies, we should bear in mind the different emphases that capitalist and socialist societies place on individualism, collectivism, and competition. Capitalist societies place greater emphasis on individual responsibility, individual effort, and free competition. In contrast, socialist societies tend to emphasize collective responsibility, group cooperation, and a motivation to strive for the collective good. Thus, the two systems adopt different paths in striving for superordinate goals, and we would expect a more collective emphasis in socialist societies.

Viewed from this perspective, Sherif's 1966 study casts as much light on the development of competitiveness in Western culture as it does on superordinate goals. The boys' behavior in the summer camp reflects a powerful emphasis on competitiveness on the part of socializing agents in the West. The mere knowledge that another group existed led to strong demonstrations of ethnocentrism, and intergroup competition eventually led to intergroup conflict and aggressive leadership. This kind of vibrant competitiveness no doubt has a role in stimulating economic growth. However, it also has a role in the historical expansion of Western powers and the colonization of third-world societies.

The final point in relation to the concept of stimulus equivalents concerns the context of the Sherif study, and the process of friendship formation around which the study revolves. The summer camp is a North American phenomenon, although we could find "stimulus equivalents" for this in other cultures. For example, tribes dependent on livestock often move to higher ground to take advantage of fresh grazing lands in the summer. The social life and the games that result from setting up a summer encampment in some ways correspond to life in a North American summer camp. However, the formation of friendships rigidly within one's own age group is more characteristic of industrialized rather than of traditional societies. In traditional cultures, friendships tend to be extensions of family networks. The extended family system means that the youngster growing up would play with others of the same age, but he or she would also have a great deal of contact with grandparents, uncles, aunts, cousins, and other relatives varying considerably in age. In such contexts, for boys to be isolated with others of the same age would not be as "routine" an event as it is in industrialized societies. Thus, the stimulus equivalent of same-age groups in some cultures might be groups of individuals with a larger range of ages. Such cultural differences probably explain why it has proved difficult to replicate the Sherif study in other cultures (Diab 1970).

In summary, the field-study method allows a fairly high level of realism, but sacrifices control to some extent. Because there is less control over variables, there is an increase in the number of nuisance variables that could influence the outcome. Consequently, the relationship between dependent and independent variables is more difficult to establish, and there is lower internal validity. But some researchers are willing to abandon high internal validity for the chance of achieving high external validity, and this is the opportunity that field studies provide. Because the field is a culturally richer context than the laboratory, cultural variables can have a more powerful impact on the result of field studies.

Survey and Interview Studies

Typically, surveys and interview studies are correlational in that they involve a search for associations between, for example, attitudes and reported behavior in the domain of prejudice. Surveys and interviews involve little or no stage management or manipulation, and seem to be the most direct way of gathering accounts of people's behavior.

Perhaps the most influential social psychological field project that used survey and interview techniques is *The Authoritarian Personality* (Adorno et al. 1950). The famous F-Scale, or Potentiality for Fascism scale, was developed as part of this research. The horrors of World War II and the threat posed by fascism led some researchers to try to better understand the personalities of prejudiced individuals. Theodor Adorno and his colleagues started by exploring the roots of anti-Semitism and proceeded to show that prejudiced individuals have consistently negative attitudes not only toward Jews, but also toward other outgroups who are different from themselves. The researchers did this by first identifying a group of anti-Semites from a sample of 2,000 middle-class, white, non-Jewish, native-born American residents of California. Their fifty-two-item Anti-Semitism Scale included such items as, "One trouble with Jewish businessmen is that they stick together and connive, so that a Gentile doesn't have a fair chance in competition."

Adorno et al. also adopted questionnaire and survey techniques to examine the relationship between attitudes toward Jews and attitudes toward other minority groups. A thirty-four-item Ethnocentrism Scale was used to measure attitudes toward African-Americans and other minorities. This included items such as, "Negroes have their rights, but it is best to keep them in their own districts and schools and to prevent too much contact with whites." The high correlation between scores on the Anti-Semitism scale and the Ethnocentrism Scale suggested that prejudiced individuals were consistent in showing negative attitudes toward all dissimilar outgroups.

In order to explore the roots of prejudice, Adorno and his colleagues conducted in-depth interviews with two subgroups: individuals scoring high on the Ethnocentrism Scale and others scoring low. Insights gained through these open-ended interviews, together with postulates from psychodynamic models of behavior, led the researchers to conclude that prejudiced individuals had austere, punitive mothers and domineering fathers, and would have authoritarian personalities as adults. Perhaps the most fundamental feature of authoritarianism as Adorno and his colleagues defined the term is a tendency to be submissive toward those in power and status positions, but to condemn and show bias against minorities and those who violate conventional values.

To examine the relationship between authoritarianism and prejudice, Adorno and his colleagues developed a thirty-eight-item measure of the authoritarian syndrome, an example of these items being, "People can be divided into two distinct classes: the weak and the strong." This is the famous F-Scale, or the Potentiality for Fascism Scale, so called because the researchers believed that authoritarian individuals are particularly susceptible to fascist propaganda. There was a high association between scores on the Ethnocentrism Scale and scores on the F-Scale. Interestingly, Elms and Milgram (1966) found that authoritarians tend be more obedient to authority.

A Cross-Cultural Look at Survey and Interview Studies

Survey and interview studies involve little or no manipulation of variables in the situation. Also, in some cases, the responses of the subjects are completely unstructured, as with the in-depth interviews conducted by Adorno et al., designed to identify the roots of prejudice. The level of stage management during surveys and interviews is also relatively low, or even nonexistent.

Because of these factors, a wide spectrum of cultural variables potentially influence behavior in such settings. In order to facilitate communications and to minimize misunderstanding the culture being studied, researchers take various precautions, such as using co-ethnic interviewers and back-translation techniques (see Triandis and Berry 1980). Back-translation involves one bilingual person translating the research material into the language of the respondent, and a second bilingual person translating the material back into the language it was in originally. This back-translated material is then compared to the original material and discrepancies in terminology and phrasing are ironed out. For instance, Wallace Lambert and Donald Taylor (1990) used this procedure in their study of Polish, Albanian, and Arab immigrants in Detroit, Michigan, where they found a surprisingly strong level of support for the retention of "heritage cultures" (cultures of the countries of origin) among these minorities.

But beyond issues concerning interviewers and translations, survey research is often influenced by deep cultural assumptions. Some such assumptions made by Adorno and his colleagues become apparent when we review attempts to replicate their findings in other cultural contexts, such as those of South Africa (Lambley 1973; Orpen 1971; Pettigrew 1960) and in the southern United States during the 1950s (Pettigrew 1959). In contexts such as these, racial discrimination has been a strongly endorsed social norm. Prejudice in such settings is better predicted by a person's tendency to conform to norms, than by scores on the F-scale, nor is prejudice associated with anti-Semitism. Thus, in cultural contexts where prejudice is normative, the findings of Adorno and his colleages have not been replicated.

By reviewing research findings from a cross-cultural perspective, we are forced to reconsider some of the value judgments that have crept into social psychological research. For example, the profile of individuals who would score low on the F-Scale fits the stereotype of the educated, liberal-minded Westerner. Such a person would score low on religiosity and vote slightly left on the political spectrum in Western politics. But consider a context such as Poland in the 1980s, where supporters of the Catholic Church and supporters of Solidarity joined forces to oppose a communist government. In this context, from a Western liberal perspective the communist government represents authoritarianism, while supporters of the Church, who would score high on religiosity, and Solidarity members, who were supported by such political conservatives as Margaret Thatcher and Ronald Reagan, represent low authoritarianism. This picture does not match the conclusions of Adorno's study.

The "culture-bound" nature of the conclusions reached by Adorno and his colleagues become even more apparent when we consider cultures—such as Afghanistan—that are fundamentally different from that of California where they conducted their study. A simplistic picture of developments in Afghan society since the 1970's would say that the Islamic Fundamentalists represent authoritarian personality types, who would score high on religiosity, probably be right-wing in Western terms, and have the rigid family upbringing identified by Adorno and his colleagues (1950). But recall that the Islamic Mujahadeen are known as "freedom fighters" in Afghanistan, and they are largely responsible for bringing about the withdrawal of foreign troops from that country. Thus, individuals who might be identified as "authoritarian" according to Adorno and his colleagues are also "champions of freedom" in another cultural context.

Now consider another central finding of Adorno's, that negative attitudes toward Jews are associated with negative attitudes toward blacks and other minorities. This finding does not make much sense in the context of the Middle East, where negative sentiments toward Jews are often associated with positive rather than negative attitudes toward blacks and other minorities. These other minorities often are seen as allies in the fight against majority groups, such as the white élite in North America. At its extreme, this situation is represented by the position of the Palestinian Liberation Organization.

To summarize, survey and interview methods in social psychology have a number of strengths. These methods often involve direct interactions with people. There is little control or deception involved, and questions are generally asked in a direct manner. However, there are also problems associated with these methods. For example, people do not always want to tell the researcher about their attitudes or behavior, and this is particularly true in sensitive issues, such as prejudice, love life, or career aspirations. In the Western context, the interviewer is perceived as someone who legitimately can interview people and ask detailed questions about personal lives. But in many traditional cultures, this role has not been well established, and the researcher may find it impossible to communicate effectively without intermediaries and co-ethnic interviewers.

Concepts Arising from Cross-Cultural Psychology

The major research methods and the classic studies we have described represent impressive advances in the study of social behavior. Despite these advances, however, there are certain limitations to the methodological approach presently adopted in social psychology, mainly because of the "monocultural" nature of the discipline. Unlike other areas of psychology, modern social psychology was from the beginning dominated by U.S researchers (Hearnshaw 1987). Consequently, much of the subject matter as well as the methodology of social psychology developed out of the needs and priorities, intellectual or otherwise, of U.S. society. In this sense, much social psychology is indigenous to the United States. Cross-cultural concepts can help broaden our understanding of social behavior—in the first place, simply by raising new questions about the nature of social psychology itself. The concept that we have emphasized so far in this chapter has been "stimulus equivalence." Two other concepts that arise from cross-cultural psychology that have fundamental implications for social psychology are the "emic/etic" distinction and the "size of variables."

The Emic / Etic Distinction

Social psychology is often defined as the study of the individual in society. The methods through which the individual is studied are designed to be scientific. In order to qualify as "scientific," such methods have to meet a number of criteria. For example, if different researchers use the same method to study a phenomenon, they should come up with the same results. These methods should be repeatable and public. Perhaps the most important objective of science is to discover "universals," and in attempting to become a science, social psychology is in search of universal principles that can explain and predict the behavior of individuals in all societies.

To what extent are the social processes observed in one society specific to that society, and to what extent can they be generalized to other—or, even perhaps, all—societies? Cross-cultural researchers from the very beginning took this question as one of the central themes of their discipline. This fact is reflected by the distinction made by cross-cultural researchers between *emics* and *etics*. These terms originated as two approaches to the study of linguistics: phonemics, focusing on sounds employed in a single linguistic system, and phonetics, dealing with aspects of language that are common to several or all languages. When we discard "phone," the root of the terms, we are left with "emics" and "etics," which have been used to refer to the specific or local ("emics") versus the general or universal ("etics") characteristics of societies.

The emic/etic distinction implies that social psychology cannot discover universals, "etics," unless it takes a cross-cultural approach. Thus, the methods of social psychological research need to be adapted so that researchers can study the same processes in different cultures. Throughout this chapter, we have argued that the key to such adaptation is the concept of stimulus equivalence. But beyond this, the emic/etic distinction also implies that when we study the same processes outside our own culture, we throw new light on findings within our culture. For example, we discover whether a phenomenon is unique to our own culture, as well as the extent to which it is a feature in other cultures.

"Social" Psychology and Levels of Variables

Think of your own behavior in any given social situation. What are the factors that influence you to behave in a particular way? These factors will range from biological drives, such as hunger, to social variables, such as the kind of cultural setting you are in and the types of behavior appropriate to that setting. At least part of your behavior will be determined by the social context in which you find yourself. Because each culture has special, and to some extent, unique characteristics, we can expect behavior in each cultural setting to be special and in some ways unique.

But in order to identify the role of culture, social psychologists must first conduct research in such a way that culture has the opportunity to exert an influence on the behavior being studied (Taylor and Brown 1979). In other words, variables dealing with macro processes need to be incorporated in social psychology. This may lead to less reductionist explanations of social behavior. Reductionism occurs when behavior is explained by referring to smaller units, such as individuals, rather than larger units, such as social groups, when these larger units play a significant role in determining behavior. An example would be explaining unemployment solely by referring to the motivation and abilities of unemployed individuals, "They are unemployed because they are lazy and just incapable of doing an honest day's work," rather than referring also to the role of structural features of society, "The government has not created enough jobs to keep everyone employed."

Cross-cultural psychology necessarily leads researchers to include large, macro variables in their analysis. Often, an independent variable in cross-cultural research is culture itself. For example, a number of studies have looked at patterns of cooperation and competition across cultures (Seymour 1981). In these studies, culture is an independent variable, and cooperative and competitive behaviors are dependent variables. Related to such research programs are studies of individualism and collectivism across cultures. For examples, Hofstede (1980) conducted a study that eventually involved samples from sixty-four different countries and suggested that individualism is relatively stronger in industrial societies, such as those of North America, than in traditional societies, such as India.

But it is not only a comparison of behavior across different societies that involves different cultures. Within our own societies there are a wide variety of macro variables—ethnicity, social class, and sex—that have cultural implications. From this perspective, we can adopt a "cross-cultural" approach to the study of social class differences within the same society. Such an approach would provide us with a new perspective on many of the classic social psychology studies.

For example, the issues of obedience and conformity are central themes in both the Milgram laboratory studies and in the initial field studies of the authoritarian personality by Adorno et al. Research findings suggest major social class differences in terms of these variables. This is illustrated by Kohn's (1969) field studies, in which he identified the conditions of working class life that lead to particular styles of conformity and relations with authorities, as follows:

> The essence of higher class position is the expectation that one's decisions and actions can be consequential; the essence of lower class position is the belief that one is at the mercy of forces and people beyond one's control, often, beyond one's understanding. Self-direction—acting on the basis of one's judgment, attending to internal dynamics as well as to external consequences, being open-minded, being trustful of others, holding personally responsible moral standards—this is possible only if the actual conditions of life allow some freedom of action, some reason to feel in control of fate. Conformity—following the dictates of authority, focusing on external consequences to the exclusion of internal processes, being intolerant of non-conformity and dissent, being distrustful of others, having moral standards that strongly emphasize obedience to the letter of the law—this is the inevitable result of conditions of life that allow little freedom of action, little reason to feel in control of fate.(Kohn 1969, 189)

Ethnicity is another macro variable that, when included in social psychological research, can introduce a cross-cultural dimension to a study. The migration of large numbers of peoples around the world has meant that ethnicity is a potentially important variable that confronts us *within* our own societies, and not just when we compare. Most Western countries now house fairly large populations of ethnic minorities. The percentage of ethnic minorities in societies that have traditionally been immigrant-receiving, such as the United States, Canada, and Australia, tend to be larger than most. For instance, Cubans and Mexicans in the United States increasingly constitute an important cultural and, indeed, linguistic force, with Spanish rivaling English as the main language being used in some parts of the country. But even in European countries that have traditionally been regarded as ethnically homogeneous, such as England and France, there has been an influx of hundreds of thousands of ethnic minorities since World War II. The result is that, for example, South Asians in England and North Africans in France now constitute important and influential ethnic groups that have to an important extent maintained their heritage, cultures, and languages.

Thus, a cross-cultural perspective may lead social psychologists to incorporate larger variables in their research, leading to a richer social psychology. Whether we take the issue of ethnicity, social class, or sex, or any other large variable, it is apparent that social psychology has tended to focus on majority groups—groups that enjoy relatively greater power and status. It is no accident that the classic studies that we considered, the Milgram laboratory studies, the Sherif field studies, and the Adorno survey and interview studies, all focused on majority groups: the respondents were white, living in the United States, and—for the most part—males.

In summary, in this chapter we have discussed the major research methods used in social psychology, as well as given classic examples of research studies using each method. We have cited examples to show that some classic studies are not replicated when conducted in non-Western cultures. We have also noted that although there are diverse methods available to social psychologists, the method dominating mainstream social psychology is the laboratory method. The laboratory *does* have a culture, and experimental laboratory work necessarily involves cultural variables. This is something that the researcher can capitalize on, particularly if a cross-cultural orientation is used to help make sense of social psychological studies and their findings.

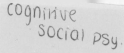

Chapter

3

Cognitive Social Psychology in Cultural Context

Modern social psychology has become caught up in the cognitive science revolution with the result that cognitive processes—those mental processes that organize our experience of the social environment—are central to our understanding of social behavior. Among a growing number of concepts demonstrating this cognitive trend are attitudes, attributions, self-schemas, beliefs, values, and stereotypes. In this chapter, we will focus on three such processes, each for a different reason. *Attitude* is, from an historical perspective, the most influential concept in social psychology. *Attribution* has, since the early 1970s, been the most researched topic in social psychology. Finally, *stereotyping* is the cognitive process most closely linked with relations between cultural groups.

Attitudes

The cognitive process viewed as the basic building block of modern social psychology is the concept of attitude (McGuire 1969). Attitudes are fundamental. In social psychological terms, an attitude is a predisposition to respond positively or negatively toward a social object (Ajzen 1988; Fishbein and Ajzen 1972). Thus, attitudes represent the *evaluative* or *feeling* component of our orientation to any stimulus in the environment. What could be more basic to our behavior than the feelings that guide us in our interactions with other individuals, groups of people, institutions, ideas, political decisions, or indeed any other social stimulus of significance? The basic questions for social psychology with respect to attitudes are: how do our attitudes develop, how are they structured cognitively, and how can they be changed? This issue of attitude-change is particularly important. Consider how much of our behavior involves explicit or implicit attempts to change our attitudes: every time we vote, buy a car, take a college course, or go into therapy, someone is trying to change our attitude. The focus of attitude change may be as trivial as the detergent we use, or as serious as our entire outlook on life, as when professional help is sought for anxiety, depression, drug abuse, or marital discord.

A cross-cultural perspective on any aspect of the attitude-process could enrich our understanding (Davidson and Thomson 1980), but two processes will be emphasized here. The first process is the way we express our attitudes toward other people; the second is attitude-change. Not only does the expression of attitudes have theoretical significance, but important methodological implications as well. The focus on attitude-change is natural, given our previous discussion of its centrality to our behavior.

The importance of understanding the cultural context for the expression of attitudes was underscored when one of us was conducting research on intergroup attitudes in South India. We were using a seven-point Likert scale, modeled after Osgood's

(1967) semantic differential, to measure intergroup attitudes (Taylor and Jaggi 1974). Such scales are a basic tool for the study of attitudes, and in the South Indian example the questions focused on relations between Hindus and Muslims. Hindu subjects in the experiment were asked to rate *Muslims* on scales such as:

Likable 1 2 3 4 5 6 7 Unlikable

We had already conducted a number of experiments on racial attitudes in North America (e.g., Lambert and Taylor 1990) and had found that when rival groups rated each other on a seven-point scale, like the one depicted here, the average ratings were usually around three or four. Notice that such ratings are at the neutral point or even slightly toward the positive end of the seven-point scale. Since our experiments in North America usually focus on relations between blacks and whites (in the United States) and French- and English-Canadians (in Canada), we are always surprised at how positive in attitude our North American subjects seem to be, especially given the long history of tension and conflict between the groups involved. What do our subjects' ratings mean? Do members of these competing groups really like each other that much, or are our subjects unwilling to express their real attitudes in our experiments?

Imagine our surprise when we used the same scale in a South Indian cultural context and found a very different pattern of ratings. Instead of threes and fours, Indian subjects were consistently giving ratings of six and seven, indicating a very negative attitude toward rival outgroups. But relations between Hindus and Moslems in India appear no worse—or better, for that matter—than relations between racial groups in the United States or language groups in Canada.

From a wide variety of media reports and first-hand observation, one may conclude that intergroup attitudes are relatively similiar in the different cultural contexts, but their expression varies widely. Thus, in North American culture it has become, from a normative perspective, inappropriate to express negative attitudes toward another racial group. Hence, participants in social psychology experiments in North America may actually be responding to "social desirability" by not revealing prejudicial attitudes. By contrast, those people in cultural contexts that allow expression of negative attitudes toward other groups, are more likely to "tell it like it is."

At this stage, we can only speculate about the reasons for cultural differences in intergroup attitudes. What is clear, however, is that we are aware that there is an important issue about attitude expression only because of research conducted in different cultural contexts. Were it not for the results of intergroup attitudes in India, we might have assumed that race relations in the United States have improved greatly in the last twenty years. The visible advances made by black Americans, as a result of the civil rights movement, could suggest that there has been a dramatic improvement in intergroup attitudes. A review of the recent literature in race relations would support this view. Since the 1940s, white America's support for segregation has sharply declined. Whites no longer support the denial of equal rights and opportunities for blacks. Racist attitudes have diminished in virtually every domain including housing and employment practices (see Kinder 1986, for a review).

Perhaps there has been some change, but it may not be nearly as positive as that implied by recent research. The results from the Indian context point to the possibility that, although it has become inappropriate to *express* racist attitudes, such attitudes still remain strong.

Nor is the issue of attitude-expression as simple and categorical as we have so far implied. For example, it may be true that North Americans follow a norm of rarely admitting openly to racism. But does this norm extend to expressions of negative attitudes directed at all categories of people? This norm is certainly followed for expressions of sexism; it is becoming less appropriate to express negative attitudes toward the gay community. At the same time, there would seem to be much less restraint in the expression of negative attitudes toward such societal groups as the mentally ill, certain Arabic groups, those criminals who are child molesters and rapists, and people on welfare.

In other cultures, it may be appropriate to openly express negative attitudes toward rival ethnic or racial groups, but does this openess extend to all societal groups? And if not, which groups require that others exercise some restraint in the expression of their attitudes? These are the questions that need to be addressed, not just so that we can catalogue the attitudes of various societal groups in different cultures, but so that the process of stigmatization can come to be better understood.

We now turn our attention to the second important topic, that of attitude-change, which has two dimensions pertinent here: who is likely to be most persuasive in trying to change our attitude and how effective is the mass media? From the host of published experimental and field studies, the emerging theme is that the more *credible* and *trustworthy* a communicator is, the more impact this person will have in changing our attitudes (Petty and Calioppo 1986). But of course, credibility and trustworthiness are culturally defined. Sports heroes and factory workers are both effective in selling one brand of beer; former drug addicts seem equally effective as change agents in the "war on drugs" as do upstanding pillars of the community. Presumably, the drug addict has credibility from being able to speak from experience. In contrast, the upstanding citizen is credible because he or she is looked up to. The point is that credibility and trustwortiness are concepts that have a variety of meanings and, hence, that their role in attitude-change is necessarily complex. Social psychologists are quite aware of this complexity, and indeed have made significant advances in our understanding of how these processes operate.

A culturally diverse approach to the study of attitude-change can allow us to better understand what makes an effective agent of attitude-change. For example, we need to conduct research in cultures where sports champions have less importance than in the United States. Only then can we measure the power of such figures as agents of attitude change. Maybe their power derives from achieving the pinnacle of success in a culture that uses competition to drive individual success. In cultures that do not emphasize individual competition, perhaps no individual would be in a position to change people's attitudes.

Also, we need to examine attitude-change in cultures where age is viewed differently. In many cultures, "elders" are the most powerful figures in the community in influencing attitude-change. By contrast, in Western European cultures, "elders" are among the least influential.

The implications of such cultural differences are far-reaching. If it is true that as people age they tend to resist change, it follows that cultures heavily influenced by elders for direction in attitudes are likely to resist societal change. By contrast, perhaps North American society, with its emphasis on youth, will not enjoy the cultural continuity associated with older people influencing attitude- and opinion-change. Because of insufficient cross-cultural research, we cannot even begin to address this issue. However, a culturally diverse perspective could provide insights that reach to the very core of societal continuity.

A second emerging theme in the research on attitude change is how surprisingly ineffective the mass media is in changing attitudes, and by contrast, how very powerful primary social groups are in changing attitudes. There is no denying the importance of the mass media, especially television, in North American society. In terms of attitude-change, however, its impact appears limited (Eldersveld and Dodge 1954; Maccoby 1980). Analyses of political debates in particular indicate that as a source of information, television has a significant impact but does little to change people's attitudes toward a political candidate. Instead, it usually results in reaffirming people's already-established attitudes. This observation is consistent with the analysis of television advertising from a cognitive-dissonance perspective. People experience psychological discomfort when their behavior and their attitudes are incompatible, or dissonant. For example, my purchase of an inferior automobile would be dissonant with my self-image as a rational decision-maker. The implication is that people tend to purchase a product and then use the advertising to bolster their decision, rather than using the advertising to change their attitude about the pro-duct and thereby purchase one product, not another.

In many cultural contexts, especially the Third World, electronic media such as television are not widespread, but they are being introduced at an extremely rapid rate. In the early 1950s, Western countries became exposed to television, and naturally people were enamored of this new form of entertainment and information. Viewers were introduced to television one channel at a time, and still educators worried that people in general, and children in particular, were spending too much time in front of the "boob tube." People in Western countries have now had forty years of experience with television. As a result, many families are actively limiting the television they and their children watch. Moreover, parents are attempting to be selective in terms of exposure, especially where their children are involved.

Imagine the impact of television in many developing nations of the world. Instead of being introduced to this powerful medium one channel at a time, with years of experience to slowly adjust to its implications, these nations are bombarded with this new technology, and in some instances are forced to cope with the dizzying effects of a huge array of channels to choose from. Moreover, the majority of the programming is created in the United States, and this leads to a bizzare experience for most Third World viewers. Presenting North American culture in the form of "Dallas," "Miami Vice," and "One Life To Live" is unbelievable even for North American viewers, let alone how it is comprehended by viewers in the Third World. And, of course, the interpretation of behavior in these shows would be quite different. Two of the authors (Fathali Moghaddam and Donald Taylor) experienced this firsthand when working in Third-world societies. From our own North American frame of reference, we learn that "good" middle-class homes are able to provide separate bedrooms for each of their children. Third-world children, who take the sharing of accommodations as normal and desirable, often assume that the only reason a child would sleep alone in a room is because he or she is unwanted and unloved. Indeed, what impression do more traditional cultures—in terms of gender roles—have of North America when many families depicted on television are headed by single parents, often with a man doing the child-rearing? Moreover, children in these American television shows are outspoken to the point of dominating the family—indeed, they are usually portrayed as wittier and wiser than their adult counterparts.

What a perfect opportunity to study the impact of television in general and its role in attitude-change in particular. Because television is introduced so quickly into many cultures, and because much of the programming is not relevant to that culture, its impact and implications should be easier to chart. This in turn might offer important insights into the role of television in Western nations. Viewers from a remote Asian or African village who are exposed to the likes of "Dallas" will be stunned at the lifestyle depicted in the show. But surely, the life depicted on North American television in no way mirrors the life of most North Americans. Cross-cultural research can help us comprehend the socially desirable and undesirable implications of the "magic box," for traditional and developed societies alike.

Attribution

Attribution theory is concerned with the cognitive processes individuals use to understand and predict their own behavior as well as that of others. Specifically, the focus is on the perceived "cause" of a person's behavior. In the 1970s, attribution theory stimulated an unparallelled amount of social psychological research. This trend continued into the 1980s with no signs of diminishing in the 1990s. In fact, attribution's impact has spread to a number of disciplines—including developmental and clinical psychology (Fletcher and Ward 1988).

At the heart of attribution theory is a fundamental distinction between *internal* and *external* causes for behavior. Did I fail the exam because I am stupid, or because I didn't study (internal causes)? Or did I fail because the exam questions were poorly formulated or I was forced to cope with a family illness that distracted me from studying (external causes)? The focus and form of the attribution theories may differ, but whether in Harold Kelley's (1973) causal attribution model, Jones and

Davis's (1965) person-perception model, or Weiner et al.'s (1971) analysis of achievement behavior, the bottom line is the extent to which the cause of the behavior in question is internal or external.

Internal/external judgments are fundamental because they point to the genesis of a behavior and lead to the assignment of responsibility and to the subsequent social consequences. It matters a great deal to my self-image whether I make an internal or external attribution for my poor performance on the exam. It matters not only to me but also to my professor, who will show no mercy if he or she perceives my performance to be caused by poor preparation (internal) but who may give me another chance if illness in the family (external) is judged to be the cause.

Attribution theory has generated great excitement among social psychologists precisely because a causal analysis of behavior is fundamental to human judgment, and because any attribution to internal and external causes provides important insights into how the attributor understands his or her social environment. For the same reasons, a culturally diverse analysis of attribution can offer much in coming to understand the social psychology of human judgment (Bond 1983).

To illustrate, let's begin with one of the more well-established principles of attribution—the *fundamental attribution error* (Ross 1977). This attributional process involves overestimating a person's traits as the cause of behavior (internal), while underestimating the impact of the situation (external). Thus, if John acted sullen in the school cafeteria we are likely to judge him to be lacking in personality (internal), rather than to attribute his behavior to the fight he might have had with his girl friend, or the poor mark he just received on his social psychology exam (external).

The implications of the fundamental attribution error are far-reaching and point to the important role that a more culturally diverse social psychology might play. For example, the emphasis on internal attribution focuses attention squarely on the *individual*—as if we see the person or individual as the locus or cause of action. This view is consistent with Western philosophy in general, especially of the American perspective—one that says "you can do anything you put your mind to," "you have no one to blame but yourself," "pull your own strings," "take charge of your life"(Sampson 1981). This self-centered focus has important consequences. On the one hand, it gives each individual a sense of importance; but, on the other hand, it saddles the individual with a heavy burden of responsibility.

This culturally based explanation for the fundamental attribution error can be evaluated only by making comparisons with the attribution process, as the process operates in a variety of other cultural contexts. Specifically, we might hypothesize that less individualistic cultures placing more emphasis on family, role, or societal collectivities, might be less prone to the fundamental attribution error. Such a view would be consistent with Clifford Geertz's (1975) observation that, among most of the world's cultures, it is unusual to think of the individual as being isolated from his or her primary social relationships. Nowhere is this distinction captured more eloquently than Markus and Kitayama's (1991) characterization of the differences between the United States and Japan. As they conclude, "In America, the squeaky wheel gets the grease. In Japan, the nail that stands out gets pounded down." (224) Initial evidence indicates that culture is indeed an important determinant of attribution style. For example, Hindus in India are less likely than Americans to make internal attributions, and Japanese college students are less likely than students in the United States to see themselves in terms of personality traits. Instead, Japanese students tend to focus on their social identities (Cousins 1989).

In terms of the implications of American and Japanese differences in attributional tendencies, Weisz et al. (1984) have made the most comprehensive analysis. They, too, refer to research findings that Americans tend to make "internal" attributions, whereas the Japanese prefer more "external" attributions. Weisz and his colleagues link this attributional difference to what they view as fundamental cultural differences in the areas of child-rearing, religion, work, and psychotherapy. They argue that Americans seek to gain what they label as "primary control" over their environment. In primary control, the person attempts to influence his or her environment directly. By contrast, the Japanese tend toward "secondary control" as a means of gaining control over their environment. Secondary control is gained by accommodating oneself to others.

Weisz and his colleagues argue that this fundamental difference in orientation is responsible for a variety of misunderstandings between Americans and the Japanese. To cite one example, they note that Americans are often perceived by the Japanese to be "pushy" and "selfish," whereas Americans perceive the Japanese as "inscrutable" and "devious." The explanation, according to Weisz and his colleagues, lies in culturally different orientations to the pursuit of control, and the attributional styles that form a part of the different orientations.

Pursuing the same theme, some would argue that North America has lost its sense of individualism and the competitive spirit that goes along with it. Nowhere does this surface more clearly than in the attributional basis of the judicial process in North America. What does it mean when a killer is found not guilty by reason of insanity? From an attributional perspective, it means that the killer is not responsible for his or her action. Accordingly, the external cause "insanity," something over which it is believed the person had no control, made the person commit the crime. The person is not guilty because the act of murder was not caused by anything internal to the person. If the person is not responsible for the crime, how can he or she be found guilty? A culmination of the fundamental attribution error may be the recent case where a man was found not guilty for murdering his mother-in-law because he was sleepwalking (external attribution) at the time.

Our aim here is not to assess the merits of such cases but rather to indicate the role culture may play in the attributions we make for everyday behavior. Is it acceptable for a man to be absolved of infidelity because he was drunk (external attribution)? Can a woman allude to monthly discomfort (external attribution) for less-than-adequate performance? Such obviously loaded questions force us to reflect upon the roots of the attributions we make, and the extent to which they are culturally governed.

Anthropologists describe a number of cultures that emphasize "fate," the ultimate external attribution, as a primary explanation for behavior or life circumstance. Is the emphasis on fate the result of a set of cultural traditions that are less individualistic in nature? Or is external attribution an important mechanism for anybody, regardless of culture, who encounters difficult circumstances? Perhaps external attributions are universal defense mechanisms for those trapped in a culture of poverty. The only way to address these issues is through a pan-cultural approach to social psychology.

We turn our attention now to a second basic process in attribution—the *self-serving* bias (e.g., Weary 1979). Essentially, this bias involves the tendency for people to perceive themselves favorably. In attribution terms, this usually means attributing one's successes to internal causes, and failures to external causes. Why did I do so well on the social psychology exam?—sheer brilliance! Why did I perform so poorly on the biology exam?—the professor can't explain even the simplest concept!

Two assumptions about culture are contained in the seemingly straightforward self-serving principle. First, it is assumed that people have a strong need to judge themselves favorably. And, second, it is assumed that a positive self-image is derived from biased attributions related to the *self.*

The universality of the first assumption needs to be examined. We know, for example, that even within North American culture, not everybody is self-serving. Some people have very low self-esteem or are depressed, and make attributions that reinforce this image and mood. They tend to see the glass as half empty not half full, and always find some way to snatch defeat from the jaws of victory.

We view such people as exceptions in North American society, but are there cultures where a self-effacing attribution style is prevalent? What makes this a particularly interesting question is the surprising results from experiments that compare the accuracy of attributions made by depressed people with so-called normals (see Alloy and Abramson 1980). In laboratory situations, it is not depressed people who show a biased negative perception of the world, but rather it is "normals" who bias their perceptions to make the world appear better than it actually is. In other words, depressed subjects in experiments tend to be more accurate in the attributions they make, while "normal" subjects bias their attibutions in order to deny a negative reality and—in some sense—create a dream world.

If it is "normals" in the North American context whose attributions are biased, perhaps there are entire cultures that tend toward more realistic attributions, negative as these may be. For example, we might expect that people who must cope with the harsh realities of nature may well adopt such reality-based attributions. This brings us to our second assumption about attribution—the extent to which the *self* needs to be the focus for self-serving attributions. Theoretically, this need not be the case. If people derive much of their esteem not from individual accomplishment but from collective or group identity, then esteem can well be maintained by attributions serving the group rather than the individual. Indeed, there is already modest evidence to suggest that Japanese students are less prone to be self-serving in their attributions than Americans, at least for certain dimensions of achievement oriented experiences (Kashima and Triandis 1986).

The minute an examination of the self-serving bias in other cultural contexts suggests a more collective orientation, it forces consideration of the whole internal/external distinction, which lies at the core of attribution theory. For example, including a person's group as a potential unit of attribution leads to a new classification scheme for attribution. It now becomes necessary to make four categories of attribution 1) internal: the self is the perceived cause; 2) ingroup/self-inclusion: one's ingroup, including oneself, is the perceived cause; 3) ingroup/self-exclusion: one's ingroup, but not oneself, is the perceived cause; and 4) external: an agent external to oneself and one's ingroup is the perceived cause (see Taylor, Doria, and Tyler 1983).

The relevance of this more group-oriented classification of attribution is consistent with the important work of Jennifer

Crocker and Brenda Major (1989), who are particularly interested in the attributions of those who belong to groups that are potential victims of discrimination. Crocker and Major argue that members of stigmatized groups are constantly confronted with attributional ambiguity. Stigmatized individuals never know if their bad—or, indeed, good—treatment from others is because of their own behavior or because of their group membership. Constantly confronting such attributional ambiguity can lead to feelings of insecurity and frustration. Surprisingly, however, it is precisely the ambiguity that permits members of stigmatized groups to maintain a positive self-image. Instead of internalizing failure experiences, stigmatized group members can attribute their negative experiences to discrimination. In a broader sense, then, there is a need to study attribution from a more collective perspective, because its impact is only beginning to be appreciated.

This more group-oriented classification of attribution would seem to better accommodate cultures that are more collective in their orientation, and where the group—family, role, or cultural—takes precedence over the self as a unit of analysis. The new classification permits the traditional self-serving bias (e.g., internal attribution for positive events); a group-serving bias (e.g., ingroup/self-exclusion attribution for positive events); or a self-serving bias in a more collective cultural context (e.g., ingroup/self-inclusion for positive events).

We could continue with a number of attribution processes and point to the potential contribution of a more multicultural approach. But that would be misleading, because it would take the assumptions of attribution theory as a given and suggest that the only purpose of a multicultural approach would be to test and potentially modify these operating assumptions. It is the very assumptions themselves that need to be examined. The internal/external distinction is basic to attribution theory. While there have been a number of further distinctions drawn such as "ability" and "effort," in the case of internal, and "stable"or "unstable" for both internal and external; nevertheless, the fundamental internal/external distinction remains. This presupposes that there is something fundamentally distinct or some fundamental boundary between the individual and the rest of the social and physical environment. But how fundamental is such a distinction? How are we to interpret the claims of Native peoples, both Inuit and Amerindian, that they are at one with the land?

Markus and Kitayama (1991) would argue that perceiving a boundary between the individual and the rest of the social environment is distinctly Western in its cultural orientation. They describe this Western view as one where the individual is "an independent, self-contained, autonomous entity who (a) comprises a unique configuration of internal attributes (e.g., traits, abilities, motives and values) and (b) behaves primarily as a consequence of these internal attributes" (224).

Markus and Kitayama contrast this Western view with the more collective orientation of non-Western cultures. They describe the perspective of non-Western cultures as "*connectedness.*" In their terms:

> A normative imperative of these cultures is to maintain. . . interdependence among individuals. Experiencing interdependence entails seeing oneself as part of an encompassing social relationship and recognizing that one's behavior is determined, contingent on, and, to a larger extent, organized by what the actor perceives to be the thoughts, feelings, and actions of *others* in the relationship (227).

What arises from these observations is the real possibility that the very cornerstone of attribution theory, the internal/external distinction, needs to be re-examined. This is said not to discredit attribution, but only to move to understand it more profoundly through our culturally diverse analysis.

Stereotyping

The generic concept of "stereotype" until recently was most often referred to as a "racial," "ethnic," or "cultural" stereotype (Dovidio and Gaertner 1986). However, in more recent social psychology texts, the gender stereotype has taken over. This subtle change underscores the extent to which social psychology is, from a cultural perspective, truly an American discipline. Until the 1970s, when women began to assert themselves in terms of economic and social equality, the concept of gender stereotype was conspicuous by its absence in social psychological theory and research. The women's movement was, and is, very much a North American and Western European enterprise. Thus the gender stereotype has quickly taken over as the most popular focus in modern social-psychology textbooks.

Ignored in this radical societal change is the fact that in most nations of the world gender roles remain traditional and thus very much at odds with current Western thought. Social psychology should be on the forefront of addressing this fundamental cultural clash and the everyday dilemmas it provokes. For example, almost all university students see themselves as "liberal" thinking persons, open and respectful of cultural differences. Does this mean that students are, and should be, open to all of those cultures that, from a Western perspective, treat women as second-class citizens? Should Western nations allow immigrant groups to continue their cultural traditions if this means not allowing daughters to attend school or allowing boys to wear sacred swords while attending school? To say "yes" is respecting cultural differences, but surely not consistent with the changing role of women in Western society. To say "no" would be consistent with equality for women but would surely not be respectful of cultural differences.

But these very real issues, being acted out in schools all across North America, are not being addressed by social psychologists. Why? Because social psychology desperately needs to adopt a more multicultural perspective on social issues generally and on the "stereotype" in particular.

If we return to the "racial" or "cultural" stereotype, and trace its history in social psychology, it becomes clear that it is one of the few cognitive processes that has been directly affected by scientists approaching stereotypes from a variety of different cultural perspectives. What is exciting about this process is that it has led to an entirely different way of thinking about stereotypes, and by extention new ways of thinking about communities that, through immigration and migration, are becoming more and more racially and ethnically diverse.

Walter Lippman (1922) is credited with applying nomenclature from the printing trade (the stereotype originated as a metal plate used in presswork) to describe stereotypes as the "pictures in the head" we have of members of other cultural, racial, or national groups. Italians are excitable, Germans are militaristic, blacks are athletic, the Scots stingy, the Irish are renowned drinkers, the Japanese are technical wizards, and Hispanics are emotional. The list of stereotypes could go on forever, because no group escapes the privilege—or stigma—of being stereotyped.

If we examine more formal definitions of "stereotype," they are surprisingly unscientific in that they contain clearly stated *values*. For example, stereotype has been defined as a "rigid impression, conforming very little to the facts" (Katz and Braly 1935) or "inaccurate, irrational overgeneralization" (Middlebrook 1974), or "unjustified" perceptions (Brigham 1971). As a result, social psychologists are explicit in defining the stereotype as an undesirable cognitive process. Unscientific though this value judgment may be, it is understandable considering the cultural context for the scientific study of stereotypes.

First, the concept grows out of the culture of the United States where black/white relations are predominant (Dovidio and Gaertner 1986). Intergroup stereotypes in this context are likely to be negative, and thus, not surprisingly, the process of stereotyping was condemned by social scientists and lay people equally.

Second, the pervasive cultural ideology of the United States has been one of assimilation, a belief that is captured eloquently by the ideal image of the "melting pot," the title of an influential 1914 Broadway play. The idea is that newcomers to America should divest themselves of their heritage cultures, become stirred into the melting pot and surface, as quickly as possible as *"Americans."* Such an ideology, that believes cultural differences should be irradicated and everyone should become "American," cannot possibly place any value on a cognitive process such as stereotyping. For after all, stereotypes recognize group differences on the basis of culture, race, gender, and nationality.

A third rationale for deploring stereotypes is the literature in social psychology linking similarity and attraction (Byrne 1969; Newcomb 1961). This relationship has been found to be sufficiently robust that the degree of interpersonal attraction has been related to similarity of attitudes, similarity in level of physical attraction and—of relevance for the present context—similarity of ethnic background (Kandel 1978; Simard 1981). Thus it would be argued that any time cultural differences are reinforced, as they would be in stereotypes, then dimensions of dissimilarity making interpersonal attraction difficult are created.

Thus, the concept of stereotyping arising out of the cultural context of the United States has been widely condemned for compelling reasons. The consequences of this particular cultural approach to stereotyping have been far-reaching. From a practical perspective, it meant that social programs were designed with the aim of ridding people of their "wicked" stereotypes. School textbooks were scrutinized for allusions to group stereotypes and well-meaning exchange programs were set up to instigate contact between different cultural groups. The assumption was that personal contact would soon make people "color-blind" or "culture-blind" and, in the process, stereotyping would be eliminated.

At the theoretical level, until recently, questions arising out of the culture-specific definition of stereotyping were all based on the fundamental belief that stereotypes were a destructive social process. Thus, research was directed at showing how stereotypes were an inferior cognitive process involving over-generalization and categorization. Consistent with the practical implications, the impact of interpersonal contact between people of different races and cultures was the focus.

It took social psychologists in Europe and Canada (e.g., Berry 1970; Gardner 1973; Mackie 1973; Tajfel 1972; Taylor and Lalonde 1987) to raise questions about the entire approach of U.S.-based social scientists. The argument made by these European and Canadian researchers was that, from their cultural experience of categorizing people into groups, expecting society to be culturally pluralistic and experiencing life in intergroup terms was viewed as normal. The result was that stereotyping was viewed from an entirely different perspective. Specifically, stereotyping was viewed as a normal cognitive process that affirmed the reality of social life. After all, even in the United States, students proudly wear their school jackets and university T-shirts. And, they appear to wear them by choice and with pride, hoping that they will be stereotyped.

The point is that stereotyping need not be a cognitively inferior, or socially destructive, process. It was only viewed that way because the concept arose in a particular cultural context, where that particular context involved widespread racial intolerance coupled with a value system that emphasized individualism.

In many other nations, by contrast, the idea of assimilation has been rejected, and labels such as ethnic diversity, pluralism, and multiculturalism are evoked instead of the ideology of assimilation. The melting pot as a symbol gives way to images such as mosaic, tossed salad and patchwork quilt to describe societies characterized by cultural diversity.

This has led social psychologists from these more culturally diverse nations to view stereotyping from a very different perspective. For example, Taylor and Lalonde (1987) have argued that "stereotypes can be an important mechanism for recognizing and expressing pride in ethnic distinctiveness" (365). Specifically, they propose that stereotyping can have socially desirable consequences when intergroup stereotyping reflects mutual attraction at the same time as each group maintains its cultural distinctiveness.

The pattern of intergroup stereotyping that would be viewed as socially desirable from this perspective is depicted in Table 3-1. The column indicates the groups being stereotyped (Group 1 and Group 2); the rows define the groups doing the stereotyping (Group 1 and Group 2). The capital letters in each cell represent specific stereotype attributes in the form of personality traits, values, and beliefs, and the plus sign (+) signifies that these attributes are perceived positively.

Table 3-1
Patterns of Socially Desirable Intergroup Stereotyping

		Group Doing Stereotyping	
		I	II
Group	I	ABC+	ABC+
Being			
Stereotyped	II	XYZ+	XYZ+

What is depicted in Table 3-1 is an idealized situation where each group stereotypes the other in a manner that is consistent with each group's stereotype of itself (auto-stereotype). At the same time, each group has pride in its own attributes, while at the same time respecting the attributes of the other group. Thus, we have a socially desirable intergroup situation where each group retains its own cultural distinctiveness, but is favorably disposed to the other group.

As soon as social psychologists from other cultures began introducing new perspectives, like the one described briefly above, it led to an entirely new set of exciting questions. For example, instead of attempting to deny that people have a group identity, it was possible to ask how people integrate group identity with more personal aspects of identity. It led to questions about the role of group identity and what personal needs it satisfied. The women's movement and the recent militancy among Native peoples in North America are prime examples of what many would describe as constructive social change. And both movements involve the actions of people who have a strong group identity, where that group identity is stereotyped. The key is that people are proud to be so stereotyped.

Finally, the more recent culturally diverse approaches to the topic of stereotyping have placed the topic in the mainstream of modern cognitive social psychology. Because stereotyping is no longer viewed as necessarily an evil process, attention can focus on how stereotyping operates as a normal cognitive process in the context of intergroup perception. This fact has led to a flourish of new questions and theoretical insights into the process of stereotyping. For example, the "outgroup homogeneity hypothesis" (Quattrone 1986), addresses the question of why all members of a racial outgroup "look the same." The "illusory correlation" phenomenon (Hamilton and Rose 1980) attempts to explain how selected behaviors by members of a minority group have a much greater impact on our perceptions than would the same behaviors performed by members of the ingroup. What is clear from research into both phenomena is that they are not simply the result of blatant prejudice but are also subject to important universal cognitive processes. These are only two examples of topics that, because they are addressed from a more culturally value-neutral viewpoint, have advanced our understanding of the stereotyping process.

Conclusions

Modern North American social psychology has gone cognitive, in keeping with the trends in psychology as a whole. Social psychology runs the risk of being accused of borrowing concepts from cognitive science and illustrating their operation in a social context. The result, it will be argued, is that social psychology is a follower, not a leader; and that cognitive psychology has much to offer social psychology, but that social psychology has little new to add to the cognitive literature.

Surely, a culturally diverse approach to cognitive processes has the potential for social psychology to make a unique contribution not only to social psychology but to mainstream cognitive psychology as well. A more culturally-oriented approach requires testing the very foundation of cognitive processes: what people think about, how they think about things, and how they view the relationship of self to the social environment and—ultimately—to the physical and spiritual environment.

Social Influence

> In India, Mahatma Gandhi mobilized the masses by making
> an emotional appeal to manufacture salt, burn foreign-made
> cloth, and weave one's own cloth. (Jai B. P. Sinha, 1990)

Social influence is the effect humans have on each others' behavior. It is difficult, perhaps impossible, to conceive of a human
society where social influence would not exist; but there is considerable diversity across cultures in how this influence is felt. For
instance, in the United States, mass mobilization would not be
achieved by a national leader making an emotional appeal to
weave one's own cloth, but it is achieved by means that may
seem equally strange to people from other cultures (Pratkanis
and Aronson 1992).

Individuals and groups influence the behavior of others
through a variety of strategies, including flattery or threat.
Among the most powerful of these strategies is *social norms,* that
is, generally accepted rules of conduct that prescribe "proper"

behavior in different situations. When being interviewed for a job at Benettol headquarters, U.S.A, for example, it is appropriate behavior for Victoria, a candidate, to allow the interviewer the opportunity to ask questions and to gather the information required to evaluate her application. It would be inappropriate for Victoria to bombard the interviewer with questions or simply to refuse to provide any of the information requested of her.

In most situations, social norms relevant to behavior exist prior to our arrival in that situation. The norms relevant to the job interview, for example, already existed prior to Victoria's arrival for her interview at Benettol. But, on occasion, we take part in developing new norms. A group of friends might, for example, develop the norm of ridiculing their peers who did not wear faded, torn jeans.

The pressure that members feel to conform to their group norms, such as wearing torn jeans, exerts a powerful effect on their behavior. Conformity always involves relinquishing independence at some level, usually by an individual to his or her peers. The peers may have no special legal or moral right to direct the individual's behavior; they do so by putting into effect informal norms.

Social norms also define how a person in a given *social role* is expected to behave. For instance, a teacher who enters a classroom and rather than teaching the students, proceeds to go to sleep would be seen as having behaved "inappropriately," that is, outside the norms that define the role of teacher.

While social influence exists in all cultures, the ways in which people influence each other vary considerably across cultures. Consider the case of obedience, as it refers to a person's actions in complying with authority. The extent of obedience tends to be greater in some cultures than others, while the ways in which one can bring about obedience differ in important ways across cultures. A leader's declaration of holy war against another nation will bring about mass mobilization in some countries, such as Iran or Afghanistan, but would more likely be greeted with mass apathy or widespread opposition in more secular countries, such as those of Western Europe and North America.

At a more fundamental level, the very values attached to social influence tend to vary across cultures. This fact became clear to the anthropologist Jean Briggs (1971) when she played the role of a daughter in an Eskimo family so that she would be better able to study Eskimo culture. Her adopted family lived at the mouth of the Black River on the northern rim of the American continent. She discovered that the Eskimo valued a daughter who would be quickly influenced by elders, one whose role was very different from that of young middle-class women in contemporary Western societies. Her Western sensitivity to conformity eventually led her to clash with her adopted family.

Such sensitivity to the idea of conformity helps to explain the controversies surrounding experimental studies in social influence. It is with this issue that we begin our discussion. This is followed by a discussion of norms, norm-formation, and larger social processes that need to be taken into account in order to understand conformity and the formation of normative social influence in different cultural contexts. Next, we will focus on the impact of social roles on behavior and, finally, on the relation of social influence to power. In the last section, we shall briefly discuss European research on the ways in which a minority group can influence a majority group.

Experimental Studies of Social Influence

Some of the most controversial, and most important, studies in social psychology have focused on social influence. The objective of such studies has been to achieve a better understanding of the conditions in which conformity and obedience take place. Studies of social influence have a history of controversy. This is partly due to the innovative experimental methods of many researchers and partly a result of ethical concerns thus raised.

The intense controversies surrounding such studies cannot be explained, however, simply by the innovative nature of their methods or the ethical concerns they raised. To explain the intensity of the controversies, we need to consider studies of social influence within the wider context of Western cultures.

A fundamental reason for controversy is that these studies imply limits to the type of freedom most cherished in the West: individual freedom. The meritocracy ideology that dominates Western societies—North America in particular—emphasizes self-help, self-reliance, and individual responsibility. This ideology dictates that individuals are personally responsible for their own progress—or lack of it—in the social hierarchy. Western societies assume that, just as factors that are responsible for an individual's success lies within himself or herself, so do those that are responsible for failure. Thus, whether we are rich or poor, powerful or powerless, privileged or deprived, and happy or unhappy, is seen ultimately to depend on our personal efforts and talents.

An important prerequisite for individual responsibility is individual freedom. Individuals can reasonably be held responsible for their own successes and failures only to the extent that they have acted freely. If we accept that it was social pressure from Jane's friends and family that forced her to drop out of school and start working, for example, then this would seem to limit her personal responsibility for ending up as a clothing-store manager rather than as the lawyer she had intended to become. Or, to take another example, if police officer Jones received orders from his superior that implicitly required that he practice brutality in following those orders, to what extent should he be held responsible for his violence in arresting a suspected criminal?

Studies on social influence seem to demonstrate limitations to individual freedom in analogous situations. Milgram's (1974) studies on obedience to authority raise the following questions: if "normal" individuals can be influenced by social pressure to behave in ways that they ordinarily would regard as distasteful or even horrifying, to what extent should we hold individuals responsible for their actions in society? Should we not shift the focus from individual responsibility to social responsibility?

In many cultures, individualism and individual freedom have diminished in importance. In these cultures, studies demonstrating the impact of social influence on behavior are greeted with little surprise and concern. In Japanese society, for example, social limitations on individuality and personal freedom are more pronounced than they are in the West (Argyle 1988). From a Japanese perspective, it would be surprising and puzzling to find that individuals are *not* strongly influenced by others. Japanese society emphasizes the obligations of individuals to society, rather than the rights of individuals to enjoy personal freedom.

The concern raised in the West by studies of obedience and conformity, then, seems to reflect the norms of Western societies. The hero in American movies is almost always an individualist, often a rebel, and almost never a conformist. While "Rebel Without a Cause" has become a film classic, a movie focusing on a "Conformist Without a Cause" would likely be a box-office flop. Such phenomena provide important keys to understanding social influence, as demonstrated by the studies of Muzafer Sherif (1937) on norm-formation.

Social Norms

We begin by considering two classic studies that demonstrate norm-formation and conformity to group-established norms. We then proceed to consider how conformity varies across cultures and how this variation stems from such broader societal factors as the economy of a region.

Norm-formation

The process of norm-formation was first demonstrated experimentally in the 1930s in ground-breaking research orchestrated by Muzafer Sherif, a Turkish social psychologist who studied and later settled in the United States. To implement his studies, Sherif took advantage of the "autokinetic effect": when subjects are shown a stationary spot of light in a darkened room, it will soon appear to them to move. The amount of movement perceived differs from person to person, so that some people perceive more movement than do others.

Sherif found that—in this experimental situation—individuals will create their own "norms" of the amount of the light's movement, even without the influence of others. In other words, after a number of trials, individuals showed consistency in their own judgment about how much the light had moved. But when persons are placed in an experimental setting with others, individual judgments converge toward a "group norm." Once this group norm is established, individuals will continue to abide by it even when placed in the darkened room alone. Thus, for example, if an individual is in a group that comes to perceive the light as moving two inches, then the same group norm of two inches will influence the individual's perception when left alone to make judgments about how much the light then apparently moves.

These studies clearly demonstrate the invisible hand of the group in shaping individual behavior. In the sense that the light never moved, the judgments made about the amount of movement were arbitrary. Thus, the group was always wrong in its estimates of movement. Despite being wrong, however, the group norm, once established, continued to influence individuals even in the absence of the group.

Conformity and Social Norms

In Sherif's studies, the stimulus was a spot of light that seemed to move; yet the subject could not be sure about exactly how much movement there was. In contrast, Solomon Asch (1956) used an unambiguous stimulus to investigate the influence of the group on an individual. The subjects in Asch's studies were shown three lines of clearly different lengths. The subjects could see the relative length of the lines and could accurately identify the shortest and the longest lines when left to make judgments on their own. When placed in a group situation, however, where other group members—confederates of the experimenter—unanimously reported the relative length of the lines incorrectly, subjects were more likely to make incorrect judgments.

Studies on norm-formation and group conformity have clear implications: the norms established by a group influence individual behavior. Such group norms can, for example, influence team members to perceive their own team as "the best," even when objective criteria such as won/lost statistics show that their team is not the best. More serious issues arise when such group norms lead individuals to act in immoral or illegal ways. Consider, for example, the norms of comradeship and loyalty that led government officials to break the law in the Watergate incident, and led U.S. Marines to participate in the unprovoked slaughter of hundreds of Vietnamese villagers in My Lai.

To know that group norms influence individual behavior is only the start of an explanation for social behavior, however. In order to explain the behavior that takes place, we first have to know the context of the norms. Consider the changing norms for female beauty in Western societies, for example. The female shape that was regarded as ideal in past centuries, as reflected in the work of painters such as Rubens, was very different from the slim forms idealized today. Even the "sex symbols" of several decades ago, such as Marilyn Monroe, would be regarded as overweight by the standards of the 1990s. Thus, the cultural context needs to be understood for us to explain the ways in which females may seek to be beautiful in a given context.

What does remain constant throughout different periods is the conformity of people—in this case, women—to the currently prevailing norms of physical beauty. The behavioral consequences of such pressures, on the other hand, differ with the changing norms. A female wanting to have a beautiful figure admired at the time of Ruben's, may have eaten more in order to achieve a full body, while the slim figure admired in modern times is more often associated with dieting. Similarly, while the idealized shape in Western cultures is slim, in other cultures (such as traditional Arab societies) plumpness is seen as both more healthy and more beautiful. It is, therefore, important to consider the cultural context within which behaviors occur to understand the behavioral consequences arising from group-established norms.

Conformity Across Cultures

The studies of Sherif on norm-formation and Asch on group conformity show that individuals tend to be strongly influenced by the unanimously established—yet often incorrect—norms of the group. Several questions are raised by this research. First, to what extent do the findings reflect behavioral patterns peculiar to the McCarthy era of the 1950s in the United States? More recent studies in the United States (e.g., Nicholson et al. 1985) suggest that recent subjects conform less in the Asch-type experiment, indicating a change in levels of conformity over time.

Second, to what extent is such conformity peculiar to North Americans? Studies involving samples of subjects from different groups show some other groups (such as Brazilians, Chinese, and Fijians) to be at least as conformist as North American samples, while others (for instance, the Bantu of Rhodesia) are more conformist (Chandra 1973; Milgram 1974; Matsuda 1985; Whittaker and Meade 1967).

Perhaps surprising is the finding that German and Japanese respondents are *less* conformist in the Asch experiment than are North Americans (Frager 1970; Timaeus 1968). This is perhaps explained by reference to the strong loyalties of people in these cultures to a few well-defined groups, their high conformity to these particular groups, and their nonconformity to strangers gathered in a laboratory.

As we would expect from the emphasis placed on individual freedom and the "right to go your own way" in North American culture, conformity is less valued in North America than in most other societies. This fact is reflected, for example, in the way children are socialized in North America. The findings of the Value of Children study demonstrate this point (Kagitcibasi 1984). This study included interviews with over 20,000 adults in nine different countries (Indonesia, South Korea, the Philippines, Singapore, Taiwan, Thailand, Turkey, the United States, and West Germany). Part of this study focused on the qualities parents considered most desirable in children. Among the choices were "to obey their parents" and "to be independent and self-reliant." While parents sampled from the United States thought it desirable for children to be independent and self-reliant but not necessarily to obey their parents, those sampled from countries such as Indonesia and Turkey thought it much more desirable for children to obey their parents but did not emphasize independence and self-reliance.

Interestingly, the pattern of responses for parents from South Korea and to a lesser extent Singapore, Taiwan, and Thailand were fairly similar to that of the United States. Why, in these Far Eastern societies, would self-reliance be a quality more valued in children than obedience? Although the factors influencing this situation are many and complex, there is a clear association between industrialization and the development of such values.

Over the past few decades, Singapore, South Korea, Taiwan, and Thailand have experienced rapid industrialization. A number of changes often accompany such industrialization, changes leading to a greater emphasis on the individual rather than collectivity as the primary social unit of concern. Among such changes are greater social and geographical mobility among the population, a general migration of people from rural to urban areas as they shift from traditional agrarian occupations to newly created jobs in the industrial sector, increased education, and a breakup of the extended family system. Such changes serve to weaken ties between individuals and the family, the local community and church, and the tribal or ethnic group. A consequence is that individuals are less influenced by these traditional groups. The emphasis is placed less on family and group membership and more on individual abilities, efforts, and responsibilities.

As a general rule, the more industrialized societies tend to place a greater emphasis on individualism and independence and the members of such modern societies tend to show less conformity. There are some exceptions, however. As we shall see in the next section, the economic and environmental conditions of some traditional societies may also encourage individualism and independence, despite their lack of industrialization.

Societal Processes, Conformity, and Obedience

Why do people from different cultures exhibit varying levels of conformity and obedience? In order to answer this question, we need to consider the functions served by conformity and obedience in the wider social context. A good place to begin is the role of conformity and obedience in societies with relatively simple economic systems.

A relationship has been discovered between different types of subsistence economies and the socialization practices of a society (Barry, Child, and Bacon 1959). Social scientists find it useful to classify societies with respect to the amount of food-accumulation they practice. Those with low levels of food-accumulation generally depend on hunting and fishing; those with high levels of food-accumulation depend mainly on pastoral or agricultural activities. Hunting and fishing require personal effort and initiative, and involve individual activity. Pastoral and agricultural economies, on the other hand, depend on group cooperation and require the individual to be involved in community activities. Major pastoral and farming activities, such as bringing in the harvest on time, require coordinated collective effort, rather than individuals working independently. It has been found that societies with low levels of food-accumulation tend to have socialization practices that favor the development of self-reliance, whereas societies with high levels of food-accumulation have socialization practices that encourage obedience.

John Berry (1966, 1967), a Canadian researcher, took advantage of these differences in order to investigate socialization practices among the Temne of Sierra Leone in Africa and the

Eskimo of Baffin Island in Canada. He selected these particular societies because Eskimo society depends primarily on hunting and has a low food-accumulation economy, whereas the Temne have an agricultural economy characterized by high food-accumulation. Berry reasoned that if low food-accumulation economies are associated with socialization practices that emphasize self-reliance, and high food-accumulation economies are associated with socialization practices emphasizing obedience, then in an Asch (1956) sort of situation, the Eskimo should exhibit less conformity than the Temne. Berry's findings confirmed his prediction.

A closer examination of Eskimo and Temne economies clarifies the functions served by different levels of obedience. The Eskimo are hunters who travel far in search of animals. Each hunting expedition may last for days, or even weeks, during which some hunters may be isolated from others and consequently must practice self-reliance as they encounter unfamiliar territories and novel situations. In contrast, the Temne are farmers who work land near their own villages, rarely needing to leave the network of paths through the surrounding bush. In order to function effectively in their respective economies, the Eskimo clearly need to demonstrate a high level of independence, whereas the Temne benefit from less individual autonomy and more conformity. Imagine how impractical it would be if an Eskimo hunter insisted on staying close to the igloo, or if a Temne farmer repeatedly wandered off deep into the bush. The former would not have much opportunity to hunt; the latter surely would not have many successful rice harvests.

Using Berry's research examples, we can identify key links between environmental demands and conformity. In the example of the Eskimo, the Canadian environment creates a need for independent hunters (ecological influence); society implicitly or explicitly recognizes this need and encourages independence (social influence on children); independence results in nonconformity. As adults, the Eskimo are rewarded for independence both by the environment (richer prizes in hunting) and by society (social approval).

While Berry's research points to a link between environmental demands and conformity, other research suggests that the extent of conformity is also linked to the type of political system in a society. Urie Bronfenbrenner and his associates (Bronfenbrenner 1970; Garbarino and Bronfenbrenner 1976) compared the influence of peer-group norms and adult norms on 12-year-old boys from thirteen different countries. The researchers presented the boys with scenarios depicting different moral dilemmas. The boys were then told their responses would be seen later either by their classmates or by their parents. While respondents from the United States and other Western democracies showed more readiness to endorse antisocial activities when the reference group was their peers, respondents from the Soviet Union, Hungary, and other non-Western countries became more conventional in the peer situation. One interpretation of this finding is that in Western democracies, peer pressures strengthen tendencies toward antisocial behavior; in the less democratic countries, peer pressures strengthen conformity to normative behavior.

Berry's study, which shows greater conformity among the Temne than among the Eskimo, also highlights the relationship between social influence and social roles, the topic of our discussion in the next section. In both of these societies, individuals behaved according to particular roles linked to the wider social structure. In the case of the Eskimo subjects, the appropriate role was that of "hunter," while for the Temne subjects it was "farmer." The impact that adoption of such roles has on social behavior helps explain the differences exhibited across the two subject groups in the Asch-type experiment.

Social Roles

Each social role is defined by a set of norms that prescribe appropriate behavior for the individual in that position. Consequently, when we are told that "John is a father," we immediately formulate certain expectations about John's behavior. Because social roles affect our behavior, those who have the power to ascribe roles to us inevitably influence us. By "assigning" John the role of team discussion leader and Mary the role of team member, for example, a teacher exerts tremendous influence on the behavior of these two students in the class. In the first part of this section, we consider the power that social roles have to influence behavior. Next, we consider the fundamental differences that exist in the nature of social roles both across cultures and between groups within the same culture.

The Power of Social Roles

The power of social roles in shaping individual behavior has been dramatically demonstrated through a prison simulation by Philip Zimbardo (Zimbardo 1972, 1973). Zimbardo and his associates recruited their subjects by advertisements in newspapers, stating: "Wanted: Volunteers for an experiment on prison life—$15 a day. The experiment will last two weeks." From among the hundred or so applicants, twenty-four subjects, selected on the basis of extensive psychological testing, were judged to be most "normal" and representative of intelligent, middle-class male youths. Zimbardo randomly assigned the subjects to one of two groups.

Arrangements had been made with the Palo Alto Police Department to arrest half the subjects in as realistic a way as possible. To these subjects' surprise, the police picked them up at their homes, brought them in police cars to the police station, where they were handcuffed and booked. This abrupt deprivation of freedom was part of the realism of the simulation. In the meantime, Zimbardo brought in the "guards," the other half of the subjects—to help organize the prison setting. The prison was complete with bars on the doors, uniforms, billy clubs for the guards, and strict visiting hours for parents and friends. Neither guards nor prisoners were trained for their roles. Once the prison simulation began, the researchers did not intervene in the course of events; they simply recorded the interactions that took place.

Zimbardo had planned the prison simulation to last for two weeks, but it ended after only six days because the treatment of prisoners proved to be much more brutal and dehumanizing than had been expected. Half the subjects who had been prisoners had emotional breakdowns in less than five days. The guards generally behaved in sadistic, authoritarian ways.

The importance of Zimbardo's prison simulation lies in the effective manner in which it dispels dispositional (personality-based) explanations of prison pathology. This dispositional explanation assumes that brutality and dehumanizing experiences in prisons arise from the antisocial nature of prisoners and psychopathic prison guards. But Zimbardo's prison was occupied by middle-class men who had "normal" psychological profiles.

But if not in terms of dispositional factors, how are we to explain the results of the Zimbardo study? One possibility is to view behavior in such contexts from a dramaturgical perspective (Moghaddam and Harré, 1992) described in Chapter 2. The Zimbardo simulation involves two dozen people acting "as if" they were either prisoners or guards in a makeshift prison. The simulation does not reveal anything about prison life that we do not already know—we already know that violence exists in prisons. But it does reveal something about what participants *believed* to be true about the roles of prisoners and guards in prisons. The surprising aspect of the findings is the intensity with which the participants played their imagined roles.

The Zimbardo prison simulation has become one of the classic "studies" in social psychology and is discussed in almost every introductory social psychology text. This is surprising when we consider that this was *not* a controlled study, as compared to the Asch experiment on social influence, for example, but a loosely arranged simulation. In a discipline such as social psychology, which emphasizes the need for controlled, scientific methodology, why has such a loosely structured simulation gained so much prominence? The answer may lie in the limitations to individual freedom of behavior that this simulation highlights. Returning to our earlier discussion on the idealization of individual freedom in Western societies, the Zimbardo simulation seems important and "puzzling" because it challenges Western ideals of individual freedom.

Social Roles and Culture

The influence of social roles is evident in all cultures, but there exist both qualitative and quantitative differences from one culture to the next.

Qualitative Differences: Assignment to a role can have very different behavioral consequences in different cultures. Consider the role of "female." This role has connotations probably common to all cultures. For example, females, rather than males, are responsible for giving birth to children. But there are also many ways in which the role of female profoundly differs across cultures. In some traditional societies, such as those influenced by fundamentalist Islam, the role of female centers on being a wife and mother. Activities outside the home are secondary to these "family" functions, and males and females are encouraged to complement rather than compete with one another in educational and work settings. In contrast, the role of the middle-class female in Western societies encourages women to openly compete with males at school and work, and gives equality to, and sometimes priority to, personal careers rather than domestic pursuits.

Knowledge about culture allows us to understand not only the behavioral consequences of a given role, but also indicates the potentials for change in that role. That females can compete as equals with males in the educational and occupational sectors in some Western societies indicates some ways in which their roles in more traditional societies could be changed. The elasticity of a role, in this case the role of a female, becomes clearer through a cross-cultural perspective.

But the perception that a role *can* be changed does not mean that it *will* be changed. The potential for role-change does not go hand in hand with the power or motivation to change it. Those who have the power to influence a role, for example, may not be motivated to see it changed.

Quantitative Differences: We have noted that groups exert influence on individuals in important ways. Throughout their lives, individuals belong to many different types of groups, the most universal group being the primary one whose members are small in number and all have face-to-face interaction with one another: the family for example.

In traditional societies, the primary group has a more important role than in industrialized societies, partly because individuals in traditional societies belong to fewer groups. A survey of 241 communities around the world showed that about 16 percent were organized into bands of about fifty people (Murdock 1949). In such societies, each individual belongs to only one or two groups and has direct contact with every other group member.

In contrast, members of industrial societies belong to numerous groups, many of which are temporary and disband after a particular set of activities has been completed. Consider the group of tourists that meet to travel together for one weekend and then disband, or ad hoc committees, or exercise classes that meet several times a week. Thus, in industrialized societies, the sheer number of groups to which individuals belong requires them to ration out their time among the different groups, while members of traditional societies belong to few groups and can spend more time with each group. The implication is that no one group, such as the family, in industrial societies exerts as much influence as is exerted by a group in traditional societies.

The Tradition of Western Research on Social Influence

Research on social influence has been initiated and conducted in industrialized societies, and is fundamentally influenced by the culture of these societies. For example, almost all research on social influence, including the classic studies of Sherif, Asch, and Zimbardo, has used more or less randomly selected sets of strangers. While such an ad hoc group has a central role in industrial societies, the situation is rare in traditional societies.

Consequently, cross-cultural "replications" of the studies by Sherif, Asch, and Zimbardo are to some extent misleading. Although respondents in traditional societies may behave in a way similar to respondents in industrialized societies when placed in an Asch-type situation, in everyday life individuals in traditional societies would be far less likely to be in a situation where they could be influenced by a group of strangers.

We should not assume that societies are uniformly high or low in terms of the impact that different social-influence mechanisms have on individual members. A society may be high, for example, in terms of the influence of obedience, but low in terms of the influence of conformity. This may be the case for West Germany and Japan, where studies show low conformity to a group of strangers (Frager 1970; Timaeus 1968), but high obedience to an authoritative leader (Mantell 1971; Nakano 1970). Consequently, when discussing the nature of social influence in a society, we need to differentiate between various social influence mechanisms.

Social Influence and Power

The issue of social influence inevitably involves power. The chief executive officer of a company, for instance, has more power to influence employees than does a secretary. Similarly, majority groups, such as white males, have more power to influence individuals than do minority groups, such as blacks and females. Middle-class white males have dominated social psychology throughout its history and, perhaps as a consequence, the topic of social influence has been studied from the perspective of the majority group. Thus, in Asch's classic study and in almost all subsequent social-influence research, the focus has been on how the majority influences a minority. Far less attention has been given to the question of how minorities may influence majorities or other minorities. However, this question is of fundamental importance, because throughout history the minority perspective—represented by such figures as Galilei Galileo, Mahatma Ghandi, and Martin Luther King—has had a decisive role in shaping events.

Almost all great intellectual and social movements began as minority movements. Think, for example, of the opposition faced by Jesus Christ and his small band of followers in the early days of Christianity, and of the hostility confronting Copernicus, Galileo, and other scientists who argued that the earth is not the center of the universe, and of the ridicule and resentment confronting the suffragettes in their struggle for women's rights. But why do some minority movements succeed while others fail? What strategies effectively help a minority to influence a majority? The French social psychologist Serge Moscovici (1985) has conducted extensive research on this very question. For the most part, his research, discussed below, uses traditional laboratory procedures.

In order to influence a majority, it is essential that a minority be consistent in its position (Moscovici 1985). A minority trying to persuade a majority that a blue line is green is far more likely to do so if it consistently reports the line to be green, rather than wavering back and forth between "green" and "blue." While the consistent minority will tend to be disliked more (Nemeth 1979), it will gain more influence by sticking to its position.

Moscovici identifies a qualitative difference in how minority and majority groups influence others. While the impact of majority groups arises largely from compliance, "I had to agree because everybody else thought that way," minority influence more often results from a genuine rethinking of the situation, such as "What that person said about the pollution threat really made me think about things differently." Because minority influence sparks an often more fundamental re-evaluation, the rewards for society can be high when we consider minority perspectives.

Societies seem to have different capacities for benefiting from minority perspectives. A study involving samples from seven Western European countries—Belgium, England, France, Holland, Norway, Sweden, and West Germany (Schachter et al. 1954)— illustrates this variety. The study involved boys in aviation clubs in these different countries. A competition was announced in which each club was to build a model aircraft. Various aircraft models were available for selection. The general tendency was for all the boys to favor the building of attractive models, all except one boy (a confederate of the experimenters) who insisted that the club should work on a relatively unattractive model.

There were cross-cultural differences with respect to three behaviors. First, there was variation in the tendency for the boys to agree among themselves in opposition to the deviant. Lack of unanimity was most prevalent in England (43 percent), Belgium (34 percent), and West Germany (32 percent). Second, there were differences in the tendency for the majority to be won over by the deviant. The English respondents were more likely to be won over to the minority position than were any other group of respondents. Third, there were differences in the tendency of the majority to reject the deviant. Rejection of the deviant was lowest in England. One is tempted here to associate these findings to the relatively long history of uninterrupted democracy in England.

Perceptions of Where the Power Lies

Actual inequalities of power and social influence translate variously into the psychological arena. For example, members of various groups have different perceptions of the extent to which they can influence events.

A useful distinction has been made between people who believe they control their own destiny, or those with an "internal locus of control," and people who believe events in their lives to be controlled by fate, or those with an "external locus of control" (Rotter 1973). To recast this distinction in terms of the discussion of attributional processes in Chapter 3, certain individuals believe that they influence the causes of events ("internals"); others, that the causes are beyond their influence ("externals"). The "internal" types would endorse such statements as "I am responsible for what happens to me." In contrast, the "external" types would agree that, "I don't have control over the direction my life takes."

Given that there are power differences between different groups in society, it is not surprising that some groups have a more external locus of control, while others have a more internal one. Members of ethnic minorities and lower socioeconomic groups tend to have an external locus of control; members of dominant ethnic groups and members of middle- and upper-socioeconomic groups tend to have an internal locus of control (Trimble and Richardson 1982).

These differences on locus of control stem from the different experiences of the various groups. Members of minority groups often perceive themselves as having less influence because, in fact, their life experiences support such a view. As minority group members, they have less power: generally speaking, they are employees rather than employers, workers rather than bosses, tenants rather than owners, receivers of law rather than law-makers, and—very often—receivers of political decisions rather than makers of them. The everyday life experience of minorities weakens any feeling of influence over events; the experience of majority group members endorses the belief that they do influence events.

In summary, conformity, obedience, norms, and roles are the elements of social influence that have received most attention in social psychology. The classic studies on these topics have created a great deal of controversy because they show the potential for personal freedom to be very limited. These studies question the validity of personal responsibility, self-reliance, and self-help, the cornerstones of the free-market philosophies of the West. If individuals can be influenced to the extent that Asch, Milgram, and Zimbardo suggest, then perhaps a person need not take full responsibility for where he or she ranks in the status hierarchy. We have to also look to factors outside the person, such as ethnicity, gender, and socioeconomic background, to explain their present status and future progress.

Social influence is exerted most by those who hold greater power. Through power, it is possible to establish formal laws as well as to influence social norms and roles. Consequently, the study of social influence inevitably leads us to consider inequalities in the *power* of individuals and groups to influence one another.

While majority groups perceive that they can influence events, minority group members feel they have less control over events. This difference in locus of control between majority and minority group members underlines the need to look beyond white, middle-class, North American society and to study social influence from the perspective of diverse cultural groups.

The studies of Sherif, Asch, and Zimbardo clearly demonstrate the impact of norms and roles on social behavior, but we need to know the nature of norms and roles if we are to understand their behavioral consequences in detail. Since norms and roles differ in fundamental ways across cultures, behavior influenced by them will also differ cross-culturally. There are vast differences, for example, in the behaviors associated with the role of female in different societies, as well as in different groups within a given society.

Chapter

5

Social Relations

Why do we seem to need close relationships with others? What determines who we will become attached to? What determines when and whom we will help, and why do people often fail to come to the aid of others who are in need? Are aggression and war inevitable ingredients of the human experience, or are there societies that live relatively free of violence and crime? These are the kinds of important questions that inspire psychologists to examine human social relations.

In this chapter, we shall explore the contributions that a cross-cultural perspective can make to the social psychological study of how we treat and feel about others. The chapter is organized in three main sections, each focusing on a major topic in social psychological research and theory: (1) interpersonal relationships, (2) prosocial behavior, and (3) aggression.

Interpersonal Relationships

"Relationship" refers to a social encounter with a certain individual that involves the expectation of continued interaction in the future. The familiar line of the poet John Donne, "No man is an island, entire of itself," seems to be supported by cross-cultural research on interpersonal relationships. People everywhere seek out affiliation with others and interpersonal relationships are an integral part of human life the world over. However, the nature of relationships and the ways in which they are enacted can vary considerably both within and between cultures. In this section, we will consider how a Western cultural perspective has led much of social psychology to focus on such relationships as romantic couples and first-time acquaintances, while giving relatively little attention to such relationships as kinship and community. We will examine the reasons for this emphasis and how an understanding of alternative relationships can shed light, not only on the social psychology of members of other cultures but of North Americans as well.

Culture and the Relationships That Social Psychologists Study

The topic of interpersonal relationships provides an excellent example of how research topics reflect the characteristics of the societies from which they emerge. In the Western study of interpersonal relationships, three types of relationships are prominent: first-time acquaintances, close personal friendships, and intimate partnerships. A cross-cultural perspective, however, might lead us to include a very different set of relationships for study. In many cultures, kinship relationships would be the dominant relationship of interest. In addition, the interpersonal relationships between members of the community would also be particularly important. Finally, in many cultures, relationships between individuals often occur with open recognition of each person's membership in a given group. The interaction is determined not only by the personalities of the individuals but by their mutual recognition of the groups that they belong to. This recognition of the importance of group membership in determining the course and nature of the relationship might lead to an increased interest in intergroup relations, rather than an exclusive interest in the interpersonal elements of relationships.

There are fundamental underlying differences between kinship and community relationships on the one hand, and first-time acquaintance, friendship, and intimate relationships on the other. The relative importance of these different sets of relationships reflects important underlying ideological differences between cultures.

The first underlying difference is that of choice. As the saying goes, "You can choose your friends, but you can't choose your family." Friendships, intimate partnerships, and—to a lesser extent—even acquaintances are entered into voluntarily. Kinship relationships and community and group relationships, on the other hand, are "forced" upon the individual. One becomes a brother or sister the moment a second child is born to one's parents. Similarly, one does not often choose one's neighbors, or who delivers one's mail. In a small community, one does not choose who one works with, one's grocer, or even one's doctor. These community relationships are determined by who happens to perform these services. Likewise, the relationships between the members of one's racial, ethnic, language, religious, or even less-structured social groups and the members of other such groups are only partly determined by an individual's desires and choices. The pattern and content of these relationships are, to some degree, the result of one's birth into a given group. Thus, unlike the friendships, intimate relationships, and acquaintance relationships that predominate in North America, relationships determined by family membership, by one's position in the community, and by one's membership in a given societal group are not entered into entirely by choice, but result in part from the circumstances beyond one's control.

The second underlying difference is permanence or continuity. First-time acquaintances are often never seen again, friendships often die, and in North America love relationships and even marriages are often temporary. Kinship relationships by their nature are lifelong. For the inhabitants of a small farming community or a jungle village, one's community relationships also are lifelong, as the prospect of any member of the community moving is highly unlikely. Thus, where the relationships of primary interest in a North American context are seen to be temporary, the dominant relationships in many other cultures are lifelong.

Finally, these two sets of relationships differ in that those associated with Western social psychology tend to be predominantly individualistic, while the alternative set tend to be more collective. First-time acquaintances, friendships, and intimate relationships are all generally dyadic (involve the association and attachment of two individuals). The interactions of the two individuals are for the most part determined by the personalities, attitudes, beliefs, and desires of the individuals themselves. Community and kinship relationships, on the other hand, are determined in part by an individual's membership in a given group. The relationship of brother and sister is contained within the network and framework of the broader family group. The relationship between community members is also contained within the framework of the neighborhood group. Thus, these interpersonal relationships are not simply independent associations between individuals but are found within a network of interwoven relationships that define the group. The relationship between members of societal groups such as those defined by occupation, race, ethnicity, class, or religion are the clearest examples of relationships that are collective in nature. The behavior of the individuals interacting on behalf of these groups is almost entirely determined by the groups to which they belong.

What elements of the North American cultural experience have drawn social psychologists to study voluntary, temporary, and individualistic relationships as the primary focus of their work? And why would a set of obligatory, permanent, and collective relationships be the more likely choice of a cross-cultural social psychology? The answer, we believe, can be found in the dominant values and beliefs, as well as the environmental conditions, present in different cultures.

Environmental Factors Affecting Interpersonal Relations

A variety of environmental conditions may have contributed to the importance of first-time acquaintances, close friendships, and intimate relationships in urban North American society. Among these conditions are three elements of the modern urban setting: the density of population found in cities, increases in individual geographical and social mobility, and easy transportation and high-speed interpersonal communications. For those who live or work in urban centers, the sheer number of people in such a small area ensures that individuals are unlikely to know most of the people they come into contact with. In modern urban life, frequent changes of workplace and residence are common. Even for those individuals who do not move, the mobility of others results in the constant introduction of strangers into their environment. Finally, the ease of travel and communication allows people to interact with others who live at a distance from them. Thus, it is highly likely that the modern urban-dweller will interact with numerous people on a daily basis and that many of these interactions will involve first-time acquaintances. It is, therefore, not surprising that North American social psychology has shown particular interest in this type of relationship.

These three factors also contribute to the prominence of voluntary relationships. It is only because North American city life results in interaction with so many people that the question of how we come to "choose" friendship with one person over others becomes relevant or interesting. Choice as an element of interpersonal relationships is also enhanced by the ease of travel provided by automobiles and public transit, and by ease of communication provided by telephones, fax machines, and an extensive postal service. Because of these conveniences even geographical distance as a constraint on the choice of those we will form and maintain relationships with is reduced. This fact is dramatically demonstrated in the growing number of long-distance relationships. In these cases, because of employment, school, or even life style, some couples choose to live in different cities and maintain their relationship through frequent (and often expensive) telephone calls, airplane trips, and other forms of communication. Thus, elements of modern urban life that result in a "larger pool" of potential relationships create a context in which voluntary interpersonal relationship takes on increasing importance.

Finally, increased geographical mobility has been implicated in the much-discussed breakdown of the extended family in Western society. In modern North America, "family" is often described in terms of the isolated nuclear family and even of the childless couple. In comparison to the extended family, which describes a household that includes grandparents, aunts, uncles, or other relatives, the nuclear family includes only a couple and their children. Much of North American life is structured around an independent nuclear family unit and many of our institutions are based on the wife-husband bond as the dominant relationship. Living arrangements, taxes, insurance, member-ships in social clubs, are but a few examples of institutions in North American society that easily accommodate the marriage relationship, while being far less disposed to other interpersonal relationships. Thus, the structure of North American life places a heavy emphasis on the importance of the intimate partnership as a source of support and identity for members of North American society. It is understandable that researchers socialized in the North American context would be particularly interested in the lover/couple relationship.

As this book has consistently pointed out, the social reality of life in many non-Western cultures differs in many ways from that found in North America. Although large urban centers can be found the world over, many traditional cultural groups in Africa, Asia, Oceania, and South America remain primarily rural, living in smaller villages and gaining their livelihood through subsistence farming, fishing, and animal husbandry. In these cultures, it is the rule rather than the exception that a person will live his or her entire life in a single small community. In many countries, the lack of fast and accessible transportation makes relatively "short" distances (by North American standards) a "long" way. For example, two mountain villages in Nepal may be separated by only twenty miles. However, because they are connected by only a footpath that covers some of the roughest terrain in the world, trips to "visit" the neighboring village are rare and happen only for important occasions. In these cultures, interactions with strangers are rare, often stressful, events and may even be viewed as something to be avoided. The interpersonal relationships that develop between different community members as they carry out their daily personal and occupational functions are likely to be of far greater importance than first-time acquaintance interactions in understanding interactions in these societies.

Such permanent residence in a small community and restricted travel also limit the number of potential friends an individual is likely to encounter. In these contexts, neighbors and family members may provide the basis for one's close friendships as well. Thus, community and kinship relationships are likely to be much stronger than in urban North American society and will likely play a more important role in a person's life.

Finally, there are economic reasons for the strength and importance of kinship relationships in many cultures. In many rural settings—where life is tied to the land—the land is shared by those related by blood or marriage. This fact serves to strengthen the importance of kinship relations. Similarly, in rural settings, cooperation and assistance from one's neighbors may be essential in order to carry out daily tasks. In addition, in many societies in which both the mother and father must work, the functions and responsibilities of a sibling can be substantial. Beatrice Whiting and John Whiting (1975) in their cross-cultural study of children point out that the care of infants and young children is often primarily the responsibility of older siblings. The level of this responsibility in several cultures is so high that these authors label such sibling care-givers, some of whom may be 10-year-olds themselves, as the "child nurse." Finally, in most societies where social welfare programs do not exist, it is one's family and the community that provide support and security for the individual. For example, a 32-year-old Moroccan school teacher was unable to marry because he was required to send virtually all of his wages home to his family. This money not only supported his mother and father, but his three younger sisters and his two brothers who had not completed university and were unable to get work (Gregg 1990). In societies where one is dependent on or responsible for one's family in terms of financial support and security, voluntary relationships such as friendships and even intimate partnerships are of secondary concern.

Values and Beliefs Affecting Interpersonal Relations

The prominence of individualistic, voluntary, and temporary relationships in North American society, compared with the prominence of collective, obligatory, and permanent relationships found in many other cultures can be traced to important underlying ideological differences between Western cultures and many non-Western cultures. These ideological differences are best described by the concepts of individualism/collectivism (Hui and Triandis 1986; Triandis 1988) and continuity/discontinuity (Hsu 1983).

The emphasis on individualism in North American culture has received a great deal of critical attention (Hofstede 1980; Hsu 1983; Sampson 1981). North American society places great emphasis on the rights, freedom, and equality of the individual. The pursuit of individual happiness and success is seen as the primary endeavor of life. Independence is praised, while dependence on others is seen as a sign of weakness or immaturity.

In other cultures, collectivism is the dominant philosophy (Hofstede 1980; Hsu 1983; Hui and Triandis 1986). In a culture more influenced by collectivism, the group is the primary unit of concern. The individual is often called to subordinate his or her own goals to the goals or needs of the in-group. Interdependence is praised and sought out (Morsbach 1980). Harry Triandis and his colleagues (1988) describe relationships in collectivist and individualist cultures in the following way:

"In collectivist cultures the relationship of the individual to the in-group tend to be stable, and even when the in-group makes highly costly demands the individual stays with it. On the other hand, in individualist cultures people often drop those in-groups that are inconveniently demanding" (324).

The general cultural attitudes of an individualist culture, where the individual's goals and interests are paramount, then, are consistent with the forming of relationships that are temporary, voluntary, and between individuals. Collectivism, on the other hand, is consistent with permanent, nonvoluntary, and group-based interpersonal relationships.

Francis Hsu (1983) describes the difference between American society and Chinese society in terms of continuity and discontinuity. In Chinese society, there is great concern for heritage, ancestry, and lineage. Ancient things are revered and respected, old customs and traditions are conscientiously observed, elders are respected, and change is viewed with suspicion and even contempt. In North America, the opposite is true. Youth is prized, progress is held as the ideal, being "old-fashioned" is frowned upon, and change is seen as inevitable and important. These two opposing views are consistent with the types of relationships that are dominant in Western and non-Western cultures. A culture that emphasizes continuity, such as the Chinese, is likely to be dominated by permanent relationships; a culture which emphasizes change and discontinuity is likely to favor temporary relationships.

The predominance of temporary, voluntary, and individualistic relationships in North American society reflects the underlying individualism and discontinuity of this culture. The lifelong, involuntary, and collective nature of the dominant relationships in many other cultures reflects the strength of collectivism and continuity inherent in these cultures. Thus, recognition of the differences in the types of relationships dominant in a given culture can serve to reveal some important fundamental elements of our own and other cultures.

A variety of other ideological differences between cultures also contribute to the dominance of a given type of interpersonal relationship. Western culture has come to view romantic love as the primary prerequisite for a successful intimate relationship and marriage. Much in North American culture revolves around love and intimacy. A look at the top ten songs on any music chart, or a viewing of the popular TV soap operas, will show the predominance of love and romance as themes in North American music and entertainment. Given this preoccupation with love and the strong association between love and successful intimate relations, it is not surprising that North American social psychology has paid considerable attention to the romantic relationship.

In most cultures where the isolated nuclear family is not the norm and where the large extended family shares land, business, and even the same home, the couple relationship may be secondary to other kinship relationships in terms of providing support and caring for an individual (Hsu 1983; Morsbach 1977). In addition, romantic love as the primary basis for marriage is not entirely accepted in many parts of the world, where one's family chooses the marriage partner. In parts of India, arrangements for marriage are made at birth. Children are often wed as young as 6 and 7 years old, in preparation for their life together in adulthood (Agnihotri 1990). There is also some evidence that, in India at least, a marriage based on thoughtful selection by one's parents can result in the couple being more "in love" in the long run than a marriage based on romantic love. Usha Gupta and Pushpa Singh (1982) asked fifty couples in Jainpur, India, to complete a love scale. Although the newlyweds who married out of love reported more intense love than newlyweds whose weddings were arranged, among those married longer than five years, it was the couples from arranged marriages that reported the most intense love. This difference was most dramatic for couples married for ten years or more, where those marrying for love indicated much less intense love.

In many other cultures, marriages may not be arranged but parental consent concerning one's marriage partner outweighs the importance of personal feelings for that prospective partner. For example, in some religious and ethnic groups love is of secondary importance. For orthodox Jews and Mennonites, the level of romantic love is irrelevant if the prospective marriage partner is from outside the boundaries of one's religious or ethnic group.

Polygamy (marriage to more than one partner at a time) is practiced in numerous cultures (Leslie 1967). The most common form of polygamy is men with more than one wife at a time—polygyny (see Whiting and Edwards 1988). However, although exceedingly rare, polyandry (women with two or more husbands) has been practiced in at least two cultures (Leslie 1967). These types of marriage relationships seem to imply a kind of "love" between husband and wife that is quite different from that seen as ideal for North American couples. In fact, romantic love as the basis for marriage is a relatively recent invention of Western society. In Europe, as late as the eighteenth century, love was not even a consideration where marriage was concerned (Murstein 1974).

The cultural differences in interpersonal relationships reminds us that scientists, like everyone else, are socialized within a given culture. As a result, their theories and research are inevitably effected by this cultural experience. The cultural values and environmental conditions in North America have led North American social psychologists to be primarily concerned with first-time acquaintances, friendships, and intimate relationships, primarily because these appear to be the relationships most relevant to the North American urban cultural experience.

A cross-cultural perspective that leads to a recognition of the importance of kinship, community, and intergroup relationships in other cultures might lead us to reexamine the role of these relationships in the North American context. Such a reexamination might result in surprising findings. As is true in other rural and agriculture-based cultures, the large number of first-time acquaintance experiences typical of urban life are not the norm in rural areas and small towns in North America. The sharing of land among family members and the need for neighbor and community assistance from time to time are the reality of these North American communities. There is also evidence that some immigrant minority groups continue to practice the family and community relationships that are dominant in their heritage cultures (Yu 1983; Hsu 1971). Lucy Yu and Shu-Chen Wu (1988) point out that the multigenerational household (grandparents, parents, and children living under one roof) is still the norm for many Chinese-Americans and the traditional responsibilities of sons and daughters to their parents continue after immigration. Finally, it is often only the middle-class urban-dweller who has access to the social and geographical mobility that is the basis of the North American system. For the poor, for members of visible minorities, or for those who reside in a rural community, access to mobility may be greatly reduced. For members of these groups, dependence on kinship and community relationships may be greatly increased and a social psychology of these relationships would be far more relevant to their life experience.

There is other recent work that points to the continued importance of the kinship relationship even among white North American urban-dwellers. A recent survey in a North American urban center asked respondents to list their most intimate relationships. Over half of the intimate relationships listed were with kin other than the spouse and children (McGahan 1986). It was also found that members of the extended family were seen as more appropriate sources of financial aid in times of need than were even close friends. It may be that although the nuclear family plays a dominant role in North American life and that extended family members are more geographically dispersed, kinship relationships continue to provide economic, social, and psychological support to the North American urban dweller.

Finally, an interesting gender difference has been reported in the importance of kinship relationships (Argyle and Henderson 1985). In one study involving working-class American couples, it was found that women rely much more on kinship relationships than do their husbands (Komarovsky 1964). While only 16 percent of the reported confidantes of husbands were family members, 69 percent of their wives' confidantes came from within the extended family. Most men, instead, confided in their wives (63 percent); many reported no close confidantes (10 percent). From this and other similar findings (i.e., Civcivelli 1980; Shanas 1979), it appears that the failure to recognize the importance of kinship in North American social psychology may also reflect a male bias. In the study of interpersonal relationships, as in other areas of social psychology, an understanding based entirely on a white, male, urban middle-class perspective may leave us with a limited understanding of other elements of Western culture.

Initial Attraction and Relationship Termination Studies

As stated earlier, in North American social psychology, there is considerable material devoted to initial attraction, friendship choices, and mate selection. This focus is consistent with the underlying premise that our important interpersonal relationships are entered into voluntarily and that these relationships are "selected" from the "thousands and thousands of people who pass through our life" (Alcock et al. 1988). Similarly, our emphasis on temporary relationships leads to an interest in variables causing the termination of a relationship: "the assessment of rewards and costs," the balance theory of friendship, "falling out of love." All of these discussions are based on the underlying assumption that leaving the relationship is a viable and reasonably easy option.

In contrast, to understand fully the social psychology of a small community or a culture in which one's primary relationships are with family members and neighbors, other topics may seem more important, such as (1) what mechanisms are there within interpersonal relationships that serve to ensure positive interactions; (2) how do people resolve or remove the conditions that adversely influence their relationships; and (3) how are people able to tolerate differences and incompatibilities within their relationships?

The more collective, group-oriented nature of kinship and community relationships, also points to an avenue of social psychological study that has received little attention in North America: intergroup relations (see, for example, Austin and Worshel 1979; Taylor and Moghaddam 1987; Taylor and Brown 1979). Social scientists who have studied other cultures have long recognized that group membership and collective interests are of great importance to people in cultures outside North America and Europe. For example, in Japan the distinction between members of one's in-group and out-group is very important. An in-group member is to be treated with familiarity and courtesy and intragroup harmony is of the utmost importance. Out-group members, on the other hand, are often treated with suspicion, distance, and even contempt (Hsu 1983; Morsbach 1980; Wagatsuma 1973). In some African cultures, the responsibilities to one's family members are so highly held that behaviors that North Americans would disapprovingly call nepotism, such as using one's political position to repay family members, are common (Argyle 1982). In parts of India, the traditional caste system remains fairly strong. In the Indian caste system, one is born into a given social position that goes far beyond the North American conception of social class. Interactions with members of different castes is determined by the rules of interaction between the groups. As a result, the interpersonal relationship between members of different castes can also be determined by the "groups" to which the two individuals belong (Chatterjee 1983).

A cross-cultural perspective that arouses interest in kinship and community relationships leads us to consider a new set of questions about interpersonal relationships. In addition, investigating the processes of selection and breaking up, we might consider how we manage to like and get along with the people we are destined to be involved with. Complementing our existing knowledge about relationships between individuals would be a greater insight into the relations among the important social groups. In the following sections, we will investigate the possible contributions of both cross-cultural and social psychology to an understanding of this new focus.

Norms and Rules

Two types of social guidelines for behavior influence interpersonal relations: norms and rules. *Norms* provide general prescriptions for behaviors that are accepted and expected in a given culture or society. The influence of norms can range from conventional practices, such as how one should hold a tea cup or eat soup; to formal legal codes, such as laws prohibiting theft. *Rules,* on the other hand, are prescriptions for behavior that are specific to a given social relationship, such as the ethical rules of the doctor/patient relationship, or the special obligations of marriage. Both of these sets of socially defined guidelines direct the behavior of the individual in a relationship and make his or her actions consistent with the expectations of the other member of the relationship. Thus, societal norms and relationship rules are two mechanisms that help to preserve harmony within relationships.

Norms. Two particular norms directly influence our interpersonal relationships and have received considerable attention in social psychological research. These are the *norm of reciprocity* and *norms of justice or exchange.* Norms, because they serve as general guidelines for our behavior, cut across nearly all social relationships and are independent of the type of relationship or the other party. Thus, both the norm of reciprocity and norms of justice and exchange should apply indiscriminately to your relationship with your boss, your best friend, and your romantic partner.

The norm of reciprocity implies that for a benefit received, an equivalent benefit ought eventually to be returned. Reciprocity appears to be a central requirement of personal relationships. If we feel that our liking, concern, or help for another person is not being reciprocated, we may come to dislike them and association and interaction with them will be difficult. One view is that this norm is a central element of human social life and cuts across all cultural lines (Gouldner 1960). In fact, Roger Brown (1986) claims that "Marx, Durkheim, Malinowski, Levi-Strauss, Homans and probably every other master of social theory identified reciprocity of benefits as a universal and central principle of social life" (pp. 47–48).

Despite its apparent universal nature, reciprocity appears to take different forms, and is guided by different time dimensions across different cultures. Stella Ting Toomey (1986) presents a comparison of the form of reciprocity common in three individualist cultures (Australia, France, and the United States) with its form in two collectivist cultures (Japan and China). She concluded that in individualist cultures, *voluntary* reciprocity is stressed; in more collectivist cultures, *obligatory* reciprocity is emphasized. Thus, Australian, French, and American subjects placed importance on the "free-will" basis for the return of favors. In Western cultures, little value is placed on a favor that is reciprocated solely because of one's obligation to do so (Brown 1986). In Japan and China, however, importance is given to the social obligation of the indebted individual to return the favor. Breach of this obligation to return favors is viewed as a moral failure. Consistent with this, other researchers have described the presence of very specific social rules about gift-giving and the appropriate means of reciprocating in Japan. There is nothing comparable in Western cultures (Argyle 1982; Befu 1971; Morsbach 1980).

In addition, there are also reported differences in the timing of reciprocity across different cultures. In some oriental societies, debts can be carried for an extremely long time. In fact, a debt or favor between the members of two families can be carried over from one generation to the next (Gudykunst and Ting-Toomey 1988). In individualistic Western societies, debts and favors are usually perceived as personal obligations. There are few examples of legal or social obligations that must be carried for a lifetime; even fewer that would have to be returned by surviving children. The long-term and obligatory nature of reciprocity in collectivist cultures, such as those in China and Japan, expands the understanding of this social norm, and leads to a broader and more complete understanding of reciprocity.

The norm of justice describes how resources within a relationship are allocated. Although there are perhaps dozens of possible bases for resource allocation (see Deutsch 1975), three strategies have been referred to as norms of justice: equity, equality, and need. *Equity*, as a justice principle, involves distributing the resources within a relationship in proportion to each individual's contributions. Thus, a relationship will be equitable if the ratio of your own outcomes (rewards) to inputs (contributions) is equal to the ratio of the other parties' outcomes to inputs. This strategy is often referred to as a "merit" based strategy: the more one contributes, the more one should receive in return. This is essentially the underlying ideology of capitalism.

Equality, by contrast, implies that the resources within a relationship should be divided equally, regardless of the contributions of each individual. Finally, the resources in a relationship may be distributed on the basis of the parties' *need*. In this case, the person with the greatest need receives the greatest proportion of the resources.

Equity is the strategy most often discussed in North American social psychology and is usually the only norm of justice presented in introductory social psychology textbooks. There has been considerable criticism of this heavy emphasis on equity as the principle of exchange in all interpersonal relationships (Deutsch 1975; Greenberg 1978; Leventhal 1976). Several authors have claimed that this emphasis on equity is the result of the highly individualistic, capitalist, and marketplace economic orientation and the Protestant work ethic of North American society (Hogan and Elmer 1978; Leung 1988; Sampson 1975, 1977).

Some cross-cultural research suggests that exclusive consideration of equity as the norm of justice is, indeed, a simplistic view. In many cultures, equity is not the preferred strategy for the allocation of resources within interpersonal relationships. For example, research in the United States found that perceived equity of distribution of resources was a good predictor of satisfaction and duration of intimate relationships (Schafer and Keith 1980). Similar research conducted in Europe has found that the level of perceived equity in the relationship had no effect on either strength or duration of romantic partnerships (Lujansky and Mikula 1983).

John Berman, Virginia Murphy-Berman, and Purnima Singh (1985) compared university students in India and the United States on preferences for equity, equality, or need in the allocation of resources in a work related situation. Subjects read vignettes that described situations where either extra pay (a bonus) or a reduction in pay was to be distributed between an excellent worker (high contribution) who was economically secure and a moderate worker (lower contribution) who had considerable economic need. Subjects could choose from several allocation strategies ranging from those totally based on need (100 percent of the extra resources going to the needy person) to those totally based on merit or equity (100 percent of the extra resources going to the high contributor). In the middle was an equality option splitting the extra resources evenly between the two workers.

The results indicated that when the resource to be distributed was the bonus (a positive resource), the most popular option among the American subjects was equity, chosen by 49 percent of the subjects. Need was the least popular, with only 16 percent of the Americans selecting this type of allocation. The equality option was chosen by the remaining 34 percent of the American sample. Among the Indian subjects, however, the most popular solution was to allocate the bonus on the basis of need, with 51 percent preferring this type of allocation. Only 16 percent of the Indians chose equity, making it the least popular solution for the Indian subjects. In this group as well, equality was the middle option, attracting 32 percent of the Indian respondents.

When the resources to be allocated were negative (a pay reduction), the need-based allocation was quite popular and the equity solutions were less popular even among the Americans. In this case, 41 percent of the American respondents preferred need-based solutions and 21 percent selected equity. However, in this condition, need was again even more popular among the Indian subjects than the Americans: 65 percent of the Indian sample indicated that they preferred to use need as the basis for resource allocation and only 10 percent chose equity.

These findings suggest that there are both cross-cultural similarities and differences between North American and Indian societies in the norms of justice. The two cultural groups have a similar change in preference when the type of resource switches from positive (bonus) to negative (a pay cut). In both groups, distribution on the basis of need was more popular when distributing a pay cut than when distributing a bonus (41 percent versus 16 percent for the Americans and 65 percent versus 51 percent for the Indians). However, the Americans were always more likely to choose equity-based solutions; the Indians were consistently more likely to allocate resources on the basis of need.

There are several possible explanations for the differing preferences in these two cultural groups. The first is based on the high visibility and salience of need in the Indian experience. Because need is so obvious in Indian life, Indian culture may be forced to adopt a more need-based norm of justice. In cultures where the minimum needs of the majority of the population are met and where abject need is not widespread, it may be possible to endorse an equity-based norm of justice. The alternative explanation is consistent with the discussion of dominant relationship types presented in this chapter. In India, the dominant relationships are those of the family and the community, and dependence on one another is seen as positive and necessary. In contrast, in North America, the dominant relationships are more individualistic, and personal independence is stressed. The resources within dependent group-oriented relationships are far more likely to be divided up on the basis of need, even in a North American context (Deutsch 1975). However, in relationships that are more independent and economic in nature, equity-based distribution is more common. Thus, the pattern of results found in the study reflects the differences in the dominant relationships in the two cultures.

In research comparing Americans and Chinese, Kwok Leung and Michael Bond (1984) found that Chinese subjects were as likely as Americans to prefer an equity-based distribution among strangers. However, compared to American subjects, Chinese subjects showed a much stronger preference for equality-based distribution among friends. This difference may be due to cross-cultural differences in individualism/collectivism. In collectivist cultures, harmony and positive interpersonal relations within the in-group are highly valued and these will be increased by an equal distribution of resources within the in-group. In more individualistic cultures, less distinction is made between the in-group and the outgroup; the individual is the primary consideration. In such cultures, a consistent preference for an equity-based distribution is likely to be the norm. Thus, in both collectivist and individualist cultures, when dividing resources among strangers, a strategy of reward equal to contribution (equity) was seen as just. However, when dividing resources among friends, family members, or romantic partners, members of collectivist cultures support equality or need as the justice strategy.

In summary, interpersonal relationship, like most of our social life, is influenced by the norms in our culture, such as those of reciprocity and of justice and exchange. Although these norms can be found in all cultures, their specific form and strength vary considerably. A cross-cultural perspective that made these variations apparent would likely lead to a more sophisticated and complete understanding of the norms. Such an understanding might lead to greater sensitivity to variations in these and other norms within our own Western culture, as well.

Rules. Whereas norms are guidelines for behavior that apply across most social relationships, rules define the responsibilities, obligations, and appropriate behaviors required within a given social relationship. Thus, a rule may define a particular behavior as inappropriate for a son interacting with his father, but no such rule may exist for the same behavior for the son when interacting with his mother. For example, in Japan a son is expected to show considerable formal respect for his father in the form of address used and in the structure of conversations. However, with his mother, the Japanese son is allowed substantially greater informal intimacy (Morsbach 1980).

Relationship rules can be very explicit and usually have well-known and commonly applied sanctions for those who fail to follow them. In the most formal case, explicit relationship rules are defined in legal terms, such as the laws concerning the marriage relationship. Similarly, some relationships—the doctor/patient relationship, for example—are characterized by a code of conduct that regulates the responsibilities and behavior of the participants. At the other extreme, relationship rules can be implicit. Implicit rules of relationships are learned through the process of socialization into a given culture. These rules are often not directly stated to us as we learn them, but through observing and modeling the actions of our parents and peers we internalize the rules of such important relationships as those with siblings, friends, romantic partners, and our parents. Seldom are there clearly described sanctions for the violation of implicit social rules. In some cases, we are not even consciously aware of these rules as we engage in interactions with others. However, compliance with implicit rules is a necessary part of the smooth functioning of the relationship. Consistent violations can lead to disruption and deterioration of the relationship.

In a given relationship, there are likely to be a variety of rules that fall at different places along the continuum from explicit to implicit. For example, even though there are explicit legal rules concerning some elements of the marriage relationship, such as physical abuse and financial responsibility, there are also many implicit rules that describe appropriate conduct and responsibilities of husband or wife, such as the division of labor in the home or the amount of time one partner can spend "out with their friends."

In a relationship that is entered into voluntarily and can be terminated at will, there is less need for the behaviors of the participants to be regulated by explicit rules. If one person behaves in a way that is offensive to the other, they simply part ways. In relationships that are involuntary, permanent, and where separation is not a viable alternative, there is greater need for explicit rules to guide interactions. It is, therefore, not surprising to find that in cultures where the dominant relationships are involuntary, permanent, and collective there appear to be more explicit relationship rules. For example, in traditional Indian society the responsibility of a family to its members is absolute. A child who cannot or does not do well, for whatever reason, remains the responsibility of the family. His or her father, mother, brother(s), and sister(s) must ensure that he or she lives as well as they do as long as assistance is needed. This general rule describes the responsibility or obligation of members of a family relationship in that culture. In North America, the responsibility rules of the family are less explicit. A parent is expected to help a child who is having difficulty but the amount, form, and duration of this help is not clearly stated or agreed upon by those in the North American culture.

In addition to more explicit general rules of relationship responsibility, we often find more specific conduct rules associated with the family relationship in more collectivist cultures. For example, the marriage of an Indian woman is a significant and expensive event for her family. In parts of India, the marriage involves a series of traditional ceremonies and payment of a dowry provided by the members of her family. Even though recent legislation has been enacted against givers and takers in marriage, the practice of dowry payment remains so common in India that it is impossible to implement the law (Kumar 1988). There are specific rules that define clearly the appropriate amount and form of contribution that each member of the family must make, including members of the extended family. Certain ceremonies will take place only at the home of the woman's maternal uncle. In addition, this uncle is always expected to make a significant contribution (usually jewelry) to the women's dowry (Agnihotri 1990). These rules go beyond defining the general responsibilities of kinship and define specific actions required of the uncle in the Indian kinship relationships. The rules of the uncle/niece relationship in individualistic societies like North America are far less specific.

In another comparison, in both Chinese and North American culture there exists a relationship rule that requires a son to show respect for his father. In North America, this rule is relatively implicit and the rule is enforced in varying degrees, usually until the son is considered an adult. In Chinese society, however, respect for one's father is an explicit kinship rule. In traditional Chinese society, a father could have his son arrested by the authorities for disobedience (Hsu 1983), and the son must continue to display this high level of respect throughout his life (even after the father's death). In addition to the more explicit general rule of respect, there are also many more specific conduct rules describing specific behaviors required of the son. An unmarried son must make large financial contributions to his parents, even if he has left home (Argyle 1982). These specific rules of conduct also continue even after the death of the father. For example, a son is required to pay respects to his dead father by regular visits to the gravesite. Failure to do so is seen as a serious breach of the rules of respect in the father/son relationship (Hsu 1983).

A cross-cultural perspective demonstrates the important role of rules in the relationships of people in some cultures. At one level, the much more specific and explicit nature of relationship rules found in some cultures serves to demonstrate the cultural specificity of our own expectations and behaviors within a given interpersonal relationship. On another level, however, the importance of relationship rules in other cultures can serve to make us wonder about the role that rules play in North American relationships. Do rules only play an important role in interpersonal relationships in cultures where the dominant relationships are permanent, involuntary, and collectivist, or do they have a role in cultures like North America where the dominant relationships are temporary, voluntary, and individualistic?

Work by a group of British researchers has shown that rules do, in fact, play an important role in interpersonal relationships in a Western cultural context (Argyle and Furnham 1983; Argyle and Henderson 1985; Argyle, Henderson and Furnham 1985). In one study, Argyle and his colleagues examined the presence and nature of relationship rules in England, Italy, Hong Kong and Japan (Argyle, Henderson, Bond et al. 1986). There were general cross-cultural differences in the types of rules endorsed;

different rules were seen as more relevant to different relationships in the four cultures. For example, the rules for close friendships endorsed by Japanese subjects were quite different than those endorsed by the Italians. Italians placed considerably more emphasis on the expression of emotion, giving opinions, showing affection, and requesting help and advice than did the Japanese. However, rules were seen as important elements of interpersonal relationships in all four cultures and there were numerous similarities among the cultures. For example, subjects in all four cultures described a fairly consistent set of rules for professional relationships such as those with a doctor, teacher, or work supervisor. This set of rules included such items as watching one's personal appearance, showing courtesy and respect, and avoiding social intimacy. Argyle and his colleagues conclude that rules play a central role in human relationships. Their findings lead them to conclude that rules function predominantly to *maintain* relationships in order that the *goals* of the relationship can be achieved. Rules operate to maintain the framework in which the relationship is given stability, by coordinating behavior, regulating the level of intimacy, and avoiding relation-specific sources of conflict.

This research has opened fruitful new avenues of study in interpersonal relationships. The analysis of cross-cultural differences in the nature of relationship rules lead us to the conclusion that any universal theory of interpersonal relationships would surely need to explain the role played by rules. In addition, the cross-cultural awareness that such findings furnish might contribute to greater sensitivity to the role of the more implicit and less specific rules that seem to govern relationships in Western cultures.

Prosocial Behavior

A charity donation to third-world famine relief, volunteer work with members of disadvantaged groups in American cities, giving blood at the local Red Cross clinic, helping an elderly couple with their yardwork, or volunteering to work in a refugee camp in the Middle East—all of these are examples of prosocial behavior. Prosocial or altruistic behavior is any action carried out voluntarily, with the purpose of helping others.

There are two broad explanations for altruistic behavior; sociobiological and education. Sociobiologists believe that there are evolutionary biological bases for some social behaviors and some have presented such an explanation for altruistic behavior (e.g., Daley and Wilson 1988). The education approach to pro-social behavior is based on the premise that altruism is a learned behavior and that it results from such things as direct reinforcement of helping behavior, modeling of altruistic others, and the internalization of cultural norms during socialization. Cross-cultural research provides a potentially useful means for clarifying the biological contribution to prosocial behavior. Data collected in a single culture does not permit the testing of the social learning versus the biological predisposition explanation, because all subjects share not only the same biology but also share a similar socialization—including many of the same social norms. However, if similar patterns of prosocial behavior were to result in several divergent cultures, this fact would lend support to the sociobiological position.

Unfortunately, cross-cultural research on prosocial behavior remains scarce. Much of the cross-cultural research to date involves anthropological and observational reports of cultural differences in the absolute amount of expressed generosity or altruism between cultures. These accounts usually demonstrate substantial differences in the patterns of prosocial activity across cultures. For example, Margaret Mead (cited in Mussen 1977) in her discussions of two tribes in New Guinea, describes the Arapesh as gentle, cooperative, generous, and responsive to the needs and feelings of others. On the other hand, the Mundugamor were described as ruthless, aggressive, uncaring, and lacking in generosity and cooperation. These wide variations are not restricted to so called "primitive" tribes. The modern culture of the Israeli kibbutz is said to promote cooperation and prosocial behavior to a much greater extent than the dominant cultures of North America or Europe. Research on cooperative behavior in

children seems to support this contention. Children from kib-
butzim continued to cooperate and help each other on a task,
even when individual achievement was rewarded. However, children raised in cities in Europe, America, and even Israel tended
to compete in ineffective and maladaptive ways. In addition,
children from traditional Blackfoot Indian (Native Canadian),
Polynesian, Maori, and Australian aboriginal societies demonstrated patterns of cooperation and prosocial behavior similar to
the children raised on the kibbutz (see Mann 1980, for a review).
These findings and others that also point to the differences in
prosocial behavior across cultures (Almond and Verba 1963;
Feldman 1968; Innes 1974 L'Armand and Pepitone 1975; Mussen 1977) provide some support for the social-learning view that
prosocial behavior is learned through socialization. However,
such empirical tests of prosocial behavior are few. Even more rare
is research that directly compares the determinants and subsequent patterns of prosocial behavior across cultures. Most
studies, like the cooperation study described above, describe cultural differences in the level of prosocial behavior. But simply
answering the question, "In which society is prosocial behavior
most prevalent?" has led to rather inconclusive results. By simply
determining that this or that group is more prosocial, we have
still learned little about the causes or consequences of such behavior.

There are a few important cross-cultural studies that can
serve to increase our understanding of this area of social psychology. One set of findings that makes cross-cultural comparisons
of altruism, but that goes beyond simple description of "which
culture is more altruistic" are those of John and Beatrice Whiting
and their colleagues (Whiting and Whiting 1975; Whiting and
Edwards 1988). Their studies provide a possible explanation of
the development of prosocial behavior in terms of the child's
early experiences and responsibilities in a given society. These
researchers reported data on nurturant and helping behavior by
children aged 3 to 11 years, in six countries (Kenya, Mexico, the
Philippines, the United States, Japan, and India). The Whitings
made numerous five-minute field observations of groups of

children interacting in unsupervised settings. They found considerable differences in the level of altruism displayed by children from these different cultures. Kenyan, Mexican, and Filipino children scored high on the scale of prosocial behavior, while children from the U.S. community scored lowest. The Indian and Okinawan children were in the mid-range. The researchers' explanation of these findings is consistent with social-learning explanations of altruism: cross-cultural differences in prosocial behavior are correlated with the children's involvement in the responsibilities of family life. Altruism was least likely in communities where children competed in school and were seldom assigned responsibilities for family farming or household chores. Altruistic behavior was most common in cultures where children must cooperate with other family members in performing many chores and, in particular, where older siblings were required to share in the care and raising of other children. Graves and Graves (1983) reiterate this point, indicating that caring for younger children provides a child with considerable opportunity to learn to behave in an prosocial manner. These findings may have important implications for North American families. In urban North American homes, children make little contribution to the labor of the family. Only small requests are made of the child and in some cases the child is paid for these activities—for example, teen-agers who are paid to cut the grass or baby-sit their younger siblings. Most of the child's efforts are directed towards improving his or her own academic or athletic standing at school, or towards earning spending money through part-time employment. Although these may be worthwhile endeavors in their own right, they all represent self-serving goals, not the type of collective contributions to the family that Whiting and Whiting found to be related to altruistic behavior.

There are several other lines of research where cross-cultural evidence may contribute to an understanding of prosocial behavior. One example relates to the finding that we tend to provide more help to those whom we perceive to be similar to ourselves than those who appear to be unlike us. In research conducted in North America, subjects were more likely to help friends over strangers (Piliavin et al. 1981), strangers whose dress was similar rather than dissimilar to theirs (Emswiller et al. 1971), and members of their own rather than another racial group (Katz 1981). What appears to be the common element is that we tend to help those we consider to be part of our in-group, people we perceive to be comembers of some social group.

Cross-cultural research has shown that in collectivist societies, the in-group is considerably more important than in individualist cultures such as North America (Leung and Bond 1984; Triandis 1972). Members of collectivist cultures are more likely to share personal resources with in-group members than are members of individualist cultures. In collectivist cultures, the interests of the individual are often subjugated to the needs of the in-group. It thus seems reasonable that greater help would be directed towards in-group members in collectivist cultures than in individualist cultures. Actually, there exists some evidence to support this claim. Michael Bond and Kwok Leung (1988) found that while Chinese and Japanese subjects offered more help than did American subjects to others whom they perceived to be from an in-group, they were less likely than Americans to help others perceived to be from an out-group. In this example, the cultural dimension of individualism/collectivism seems to be an important mediator of the in-group or similarity effect in altruistic behavior.

Another interesting area where cross-cultural research may contribute to our understanding of prosocial behavior is in the psychology of receiving aid. The psychology of the aid recipient has not been a major focus for social psychological study. The reaction of the recipient was assumed to be positive. After all, seeking and receiving help usually results in increased material benefits for the recipient. However, there is increasing evidence that the reaction to being helped may be much more negative than assumed. Some of this evidence comes from cross-cultural work research on the reactions of recipients to foreign aid.

The factor that may be the most important in determining the response to aid appears to be the characteristics of the donor (Gergen and Gergen 1974). In an effort to investigate the importance of the donor, Kenneth and Mary Gergen examined public-opinion surveys in a number of aid-receiving nations with divergent cultures (e.g., Iran, Brazil, India, and Uruguay). They found that the perceived motive of the donor was important. When the native populations of these countries perceived that the aid was provided in good will with real concern for the recipient, they indicated greater appreciation and acceptance of both the aid and the donor. In addition, they found a correlation between the perceived attractiveness of the donor nation and appreciation and acceptance of the aid. Even when the amount and type of aid was the same, when the donor nation was perceived in terms that were attractive to the recipient nation, the aid was considered more valuable and was better received. For example, if the New Russian Republic is seen as imperialistic in Turkey, its aid programs are not well-received. Similarly, if minority groups in the United States are perceived to be suffering, this has negative implications for the response to American aid in such countries as Brazil, Nigeria, and Senegal. Finally, the wealth of the donor was negatively correlated with appreciation and liking of the donor. Aid from relatively poorer nations was accorded more value and the donor was seen as more attractive than similar aid from a wealth nation.

The second factor that seems to be important is the characteristics of the benefit itself. There is some evidence that people appreciate assistance more when there is an opportunity or even an obligation to reciprocate (Castro 1974; Clark et al. 1974). When there is no opportunity to repay the helper, the recipient may feel negatively towards both the aid and the helper. Laboratory research in Sweden, Japan, and the United States supports the cross-cultural generality of this finding (Gergen et al. 1974). It may be the inability of recipient nations to return the favor that, in part, explains the anti-American sentiment in nations that are now receiving or have received aid from the United States. In addition, aid that is given in a manner that implies incompetence or a lack of capability on the part of the recipient can have negative effects on the recipient's self-esteem (Morse 1972). The effect of aid that reduces self-esteem seems to vary across cultures. In Scotland, the United States, Korea, and South

Africa, patronizing aid was greeted with distaste and contempt for the donor. However, Japanese and Chinese recipients were somewhat less negatively affected by such aid. Gergen and his colleagues (1980) propose that Buddhist teachings in these countries, which strongly condemn self-centered attitudes and efforts to build one's own esteem, may reduce the effect of esteem-reducing forms of aid.

Characteristics of the aid recipients themselves can affect their reactions to the aid they receive (Gergen et al. 1980). The recipient's need for autonomy (independence) is an important determinant of reaction to aid. If aid leads the recipient to feel dependent on the donor, it is unlikely to be well-received and the donor is unlikely to be perceived as attractive. One strategy to avoid threatening the autonomy of aid-receiving nations is to give the recipient as much control as possible over the form that the aid will take and how it will be used.

The research of Gergen and his colleagues (1980), Bond and Leung (1988), and Whiting and Whiting (1975) provides us with cross-cultural research that attempts to determine how particular elements of culture are involved in giving and receiving help. These programs of research are useful, not only in establishing or improving the cultural generality of our understanding of altruism, but also may suggest ways to increase the amount of prosocial behavior in our own societies.

Aggression

As with prosocial behavior, there are both biological and social-learning explanations for aggressive behavior. A biological explanation for aggressive behavior would predict similarities in aggressive behavior across cultural lines, while an explanation based on social learning and the influences of socialization would predict differences. There is some evidence that certain biological factors, such as the level of the male hormone testosterone (Mazur 1985), may predispose individuals to react more or less aggressively. However, as with prosocial behavior, much of the cross-cultural evidence points to the diversity of cultural norms and values concerning aggression. For example, the Inuit of the North American Arctic have been described as a peace-loving group, as have the Pygmies of Africa and the Amerindian tribes of Zuni and Blackfoot. Anthropological reports indicate that, in these societies, controversy is avoided; conflicts resolved through withdrawal or negotiation; physical violence is rare; and war against neighboring communities, almost nonexistent (Gorer 1986). Gorer describes several common cultural characteristics of these societies. They tend to consist of smaller groups, isolated from other groups. They do not need or have a warrior caste and have reacted to encroachment by others by retreating to even more remote areas. These societies do not idealize bravery or aggressiveness as a sign of masculinity and do not have aggressive religious gods. These cultures seem to have values and norms which promote a happy, guilt-free existence.

At the other end of the spectrum, we find the Yanomano of the Upper Amazon region of South America. Chagnon (1974) was the first anthropologist to study these fierce and violent people. He describes a society where there is almost constant warfare between villages, where fighting and argument within villages occur almost as frequently, where men proudly display their scars of battles and where a man's love for his wife is measured by the harshness of the beatings she receives. Chagnon estimates that one-third of the male population in this group die violent deaths. Bravery is revered, aggressiveness is the primary determinant of status and position, and disputes are resolved through violent confrontation.

Influence of other, primarily Western, cultures resulted in considerable change in the cultures of many of these societies and has modified the values and norms (Alcock et al. 1988). However, the existence of the highly peaceable societies and their dramatic difference from such warlike societies as the Yanomano points to the importance of cultural norms and values in the amount and expression of aggression.

Cross-cultural differences in aggressive behavior are not limited to so called primitive tribes. The Mennonites, the Amish, and the Hutterites provide examples of groups in contemporary society that have strong norms and values against violence, resulting in societies where interpersonal aggression is almost unknown (Bandura and Walters 1963). The nonaggressive behavior of members of these groups is in stark contrast to the growing violence in the dominant Western culture surrounding them.

In Japanese culture, parents actively discourage quarreling and encourage their children to yield rather than fight on. When Japanese children are faced with an argument or a fight, their mother will likely tell them *Makeru ga kachi*, which means "To lose is to win." In the Japanese household, the child who yields is honored (Alcock et al. 1988). Compare this with the common North American teaching of "Stand up for yourself," and "If he hits you, hit him back." Such different socialization practices are likely to lead to very different attitudes towards aggression. Consistent with this, Carlson and Miller (1988)—after reviewing research on aggression—concluded that in Western societies the "dominant response" to an insult is "to counteraggress." On the other hand, in many cultures the norm is to avoid, comply with, or "paper-over" potential conflicts and withdraw or ignore aggressive challenges or insults (Triandis et al. 1988). For example, North American Native Indians have developed a distaste for Western assertiveness and tend to avoid those who interact in assertive ways (More 1985).

A number of psychologists have attempted to apply the rigors of psychological research to further explore some of the findings of anthropological observation. Researchers in Poland (Fraczek 1985) and Finland (Lagerspetz and Westman 1980) found that Poles and Finns were similar in the types of aggressive acts they engaged in and the justifications they used for aggression that they found acceptable. However, Poles found a greater number of aggressive acts to be acceptable and generally found aggression to be more justifiable than did the Finnish sample. Although this is a single cross-cultural comparison and both are European cultures, the findings suggest that there are cultural differences in attitudes towards aggression that could result in differing levels of aggression in different societies.

Although diversity across cultures indicates the importance of recognizing culture as a variable in any discussion of human aggression, it also serves to support some social psychological principles that have been found through North American research. Western research investigating how aggressive behavior might be learned has shown that positive reinforcement of aggressive behavior can teach people to be more aggressive (Baron 1977). In addition, Western studies of family life have shown that parents who encourage, approve of, and reward aggressive behavior bring up children who exhibit more aggressive behavior (Bandura 1973). The examination of practices in other cultures lends support to this social-learning explanation. The culture of the fierce Yanomano rewards aggressive behavior; the pacifist norms of the Inuit do not. Moreover, in societies where aggression is encouraged and rewarded, we find evidence of greater levels of aggressive behavior.

The findings of Whiting and Whiting's (1975) Six Cultures study, discussed earlier in the Prosocial Behavior section of this chapter, has been used by several researchers to examine aggressive behavior in children cross-culturally. William Lambert (1971) reported differences across these six communities (a rural tribal group in Nyansongo, Kenya; a caste group in Northern India; a Native village in Mexico; the Okinawan village of Taira; a Philippine barrio on the island of Luzon; and a New England Baptist community in the United States) in the level to which parents would punish aggressive behavior by their children directed at either other children or the child's mother. The Mexican parents were the most punitive for aggression against other children, while the American parents stand out as particularly tolerant of aggression against other children. Lambert suggests that these differences are due to the presence or absence of close relatives in the child's play group and the level of interdependence of the extended family that leads to greater adult control over childhood control. One Mexican mother described it this way: "I cannot permit my son to fight with the child next door in the Mexican town, because he is my brother's child and if our children don't get along, then my brother and I may come to a parting of the ways and that may lead to great problems" (Lambert 1971, 51).

This interpretation is also supported by findings for mother-directed aggression. The Kenyan mothers were most punishing with their children for aggression directed at them. The Kenyan households are also those most likely to have extra adults living there. Lambert proposes that the punitiveness arises out of the reasonable fear that a child who is aggressive with his own mother will also be aggressive against the other adults in the home. As one Kenyan mother explains: "Would it be wise to let my son develop the habit of hitting me if there is a chance that he will then hit his grandfather? Particularly if his grandfather owns the house I live in?" The relatively high tolerance of peer-directed aggression by the U.S. parents is also consistent with this interpretation. In the U.S. community, there were few relatives living nearby and little interaction with neighbors, and American parents showed considerably lower concern for fighting between children. Under conditions of interdependence and high-density living, according to this interpretation, the need to control aggression increases. Therefore, parents take a stronger punitive position with regards to their child's aggressive behavior.

Beyond this interpretation, it seems that the relative lack of concern about peer-directed aggression by American mothers reflected the cultural values examined earlier in our discussion of interpersonal relationships. For example, one mother said, "If he can't get along with one child, he can always play with someone else. There are many children around to *choose* from" (italics added). This statement clearly reflects the attitude that interpersonal relationships are the product of choice and can be terminated. Given this element of choice and impermanence, it is less consequential to be aggressive against those around you. The quotations of the Mexican and Kenyan mothers given above reflect the importance placed on the permanence of interpersonal relationships. Parting ways with one's brother or one's father-in-law is recognized as a problematic situation that must be avoided at all costs.

Ruth and Robert Munroe (Munroe and Munroe 1975) re-examined the Six Culture data and, like Lambert, they found that the presence of extended families and interdependence of neighboring families leads to greater punishment of children's aggression. They also noted that this parental approach appears inconsistent with most findings of Western research consistently showing that the use of punishment results in increased aggressiveness, not less. Their re-examination showed that, in fact, the societies with extended-family households not only had the highest levels of parental punishment of aggression, but they also had the highest level of childhood aggression. Thus, the extended family not only treats aggression harshly but also breeds aggression. Hence, the cross-cultural examination of these six different societies served not only to demonstrate the diversity of norms concerning childhood aggression, but also the consistency of one potential explanation as demonstrated in North American research.

Perhaps the strongest cross-cultural principle of aggression is that males display more aggression than females. This is perhaps the most consistent and most documented cross-cultural finding (Ember 1981). Virtually all anthropological studies find more incidents of male than female aggression. The Six Cultures study consistently found boys to be more aggressive than girls. Cross-cultural studies of criminal behavior also support this gender difference. In all forty-eight nonindustrialized societies for which information on crime was available in the Human Relations Area files (Bacon et al. 1963), males committed by far the greatest number of violent criminal acts. Marshall Segall (1988) in a review of cross-cultural contributions to the social psychology of aggression concludes that "It is virtually impossible to find a society in which young girls are more aggressive than young boys" (p. 211). The consistency of this finding clearly implicates the possibility of a biological cause. As we mentioned earlier, there is evidence that ties the male hormone of testosterone to aggressive behavior. Segall, on the other hand, proposes a biocultural interaction model proposing that male biological predisposition to aggression interacts with cultural mechanisms to produce the consistent sex difference in aggressive behavior. One mechanism is that in many cultures boys are deliberately taught and encouraged to behave aggressively more so than are girls (Barry et al. 1976). However, Segall proposes that much of the greater aggressiveness demonstrated by males can be described as compensatory macho, resulting from the male's need to affirm his male identity and to display clearly that he is acting like an adult male. This pattern is also referred to as gender-marking behavior (Whiting 1965), and the particular need for males to engage in such behavior results from their having been raised almost exclusively by women. Almost universally, child-rearing is the job of women and, because male children are often separated from the men of the society during their childhood, as they become independent from their mothers they will need to establish their identity as an adult male. In societies where part of the male identity includes some level of aggressive behavior, these young males will exaggerate such behavior in order to clearly establish their manhood.

Support for this model of aggression is provided by research showing that aggressive crimes such as assaults, rapes, and murders were more apt to occur in societies where fathers are not active participants in child-rearing and where early mother-son bonds are very strong (Bacon et al. 1963). More research is necessary in order to fully test the model. However, it does have interesting implications for the potential benefits of an increased role for fathers in child-rearing and the inclusion of males in early childhood services, such as daycare and primary school education.

Summary and Conclusions

The importance of social relations is not bound by culture. Human beings are social animals and how we interact with those around us is a universal concern. However, there are substantial cross-cultural differences in human interaction: the type of relationships dominant in people's lives and the specific responsibilities and behaviors appropriate in a given relationship. Awareness of these cross-cultural differences can improve our understanding of the social psychology of interpersonal relationships. Cross-cultural studies that demonstrate the importance of kinship, community, and intergroup relationship in many non-Western cultures not only describe an interesting element of these cultures but focus attention on the limitations of the set of relationships usually studied by Western social psychology. It appears that an understanding of kinship and community relationships may be highly relevant to many groups within North American culture.

Cross-cultural research on human aggression and prosocial behavior points clearly to the diversity of norms and characteristic levels of such behaviors. Despite the clear differences we find between cultures, the research in other cultures also points to some pan-cultural generalities, such as the almost universal tendency for males to be more aggressive than females. Research in a variety of societies has also provided some support for several principles of aggression and prosocial behavior developed through Western research. Examples are the correlation between punitive parenting and increased aggressive behavior in children and the relationship or the correlation between opportunity to reciprocate and liking for a helper. The study of human aggression and altruism is an enlightening example of how cross-cultural research can provide us with an increased appreciation for the diversity of human societies, while at the same time providing a valuable tool to test the principle and theories generated through research in a single or limited cultural setting.

6

Intercultural Contact and Social Psychology

Many of the basic social psychological processes highlighted in the earlier chapters of this book are eminently applicable to important social issues. Increasingly, social psychologists are applying their theories and research findings in social cognition, social influence, and social relations to important "real-world" phenomena. Knowledge acquired through social psychological research is being brought to bear on areas such as health, the justice system, business, and the mass media. The theme of this text has been how a cross-cultural perspective can strengthen and enrich the study of social psychology. In applying this theme, the central issue of this chapter is contact between cultures. The combined contributions of research in social and cross-cultural psychology have much to offer in describing, explaining, and perhaps facilitating the processes and in solving the problems that arise when people from diverse cultures come into contact.

Historically, interaction between culturally diverse groups has been limited. Distance and environmental conditions served to prevent most members of one cultural group from coming face to face with people of other cultures. Intercultural contact was the province of the explorer, the soldier, the diplomat, or the merchant. When two cultural groups did come to share a common geographical area, such as Native peoples and Europeans in North America or Australia, or blacks and whites in South Africa and the United States, social forces often served to prevent interpersonal interaction between culturally divergent groups almost as effectively as had geographical distance. These social forces usually took one of two forms: segregation or assimilation.

Segregation was (and still is) based on the perception that the mixing of different cultural groups should be avoided. It involves policies intended to limit contact between cultural groups. Institutions such as apartheid in South Africa, Native reservations, and "separate but equal" education for blacks and whites in the United States are examples of cultural segregation enshrined into law. These and similar policies resulted in little interpersonal contact between members of these divergent cultural groups. Segregation was enforced not only by social institutions and laws, but also by the attitudes and beliefs held by the people themselves. In many societies, the segregation of culturally divergent groups was perceived as appropriate and individuals chose to avoid interaction with members of other groups. In North America, the development of ethnic "ghettos" was (and in many places still is) seen as appropriate. Newcomers were discouraged from settling in areas of town where they didn't "belong." In addition, cultural segregation was not limited to where one chose to live. Many educational institutions and employment practices served to reinforce cultural segregation. Such segregation of culturally divergent groups is by no means exclusive to North America. Ethnic and culturally segregated neighborhoods and schools have tended to be the rule rather than the exception the world over. In Europe, Turkish "guest workers" were strongly encouraged (or even forced) to reside in established camps or dormitories and were allowed to take only specific jobs. Korean immigrants to Japan are quite segregated from the majority Japanese population.

Assimilation, on the other hand, involves the perception that members of divergent cultural groups should discard their heritage culture and take on the culture of the majority group. The American concept of a melting pot has come to represent this assimilationist orientation. Immigrants coming to the United States are expected to abandon their "old" culture and accept the "American way." Laws that require immigrants to renounce other citizenships, study American history, and advocate American beliefs in the form of pledges and oaths represent institutionalized efforts to assimilate immigrants. Like segregation, assimilation has also been supported by the attitudes and beliefs held by people themselves. Members of the majority culture in many countries have been intolerant of those who express attitudes or engage in behaviors different from their own. The education system and the media are subtle ways to "teach" the dominant culture to minority groups. However, there are also some not-so-subtle ways of persuading members of other cultures to join the majority, such as discrimination, aggression, and violence against those who will not conform.

Thus, for much of human history geographical distance, or institutionalized segregation and assimilation—and the attitudes supporting each of them—have combined to successfully limit the amount of interpersonal interaction between members of different cultural groups. This lack of interpersonal contact created little general interest in cultural differences. With groups either living isolated from one another, or minority groups abandoning their divergent cultures, there was little interest in the study of cross-cultural contact. Today, however, cultural isolation is the exception rather than the rule. The restrictions of geographical distance have been reduced substantially by high-speed transportation and telecommunications. Many North Americans and Europeans travel to places with cultures very different from their own—most often for pleasure but also for business, education, or even permanent relocation. Gone are the days where only the diplomats, missionaries, and the military were sent to far-away places.

In addition, complementing the growing number of North Americans and Western Europeans who visit other cultures, changing patterns of immigration bring increased numbers of people from many non-European cultures into North America and Western Europe. Beyond their traditional exchange of tourists, North America and Europe are now host to record numbers of Japanese and other Asian tourists. International student exchanges and international business interests bring many people from a wide variety of divergent cultures to North America, often for relatively lengthy periods. Recent trends have seen the traditional flow of Western European immigrants outnumbered by immigrants and refugees from other parts of the world (see Taylor 1991). In the big cities of North America (and to an increasing degree in the smaller town), one can find large numbers of people who speak a language other than English and who have values, beliefs, and norms for behavior that are very different from the majority North America culture.

Many of the barriers that traditionally separated groups living within North American and European societies are fading, as well. The institution of programs to desegregate schools and neighborhoods and efforts to increase diversity in the workplace through affirmative action are examples of policies in North America designed to reduce some of the barriers that until recently separated ethnic and cultural groups. Today, it is far more likely than it was just a couple of decades ago that people will live and work in a culturally heterogeneous environment.

In present-day North American society and for most societies the world over, travel and migration, international trade and the growth of multinational companies, mass communication and the mass media, as well as desegregation and integration have all combined to create a situation where contact between people from different cultures has become part of everyday life. However, increased contact has not necessarily led to increased understanding or liking. Prejudice, discrimination, and intergroup conflict are the most dramatic examples of this lack of understanding and represent serious problems in any multicultural context. However, even simple failure to recognize and show sensitivity for cultural differences can result in less dramatic, but no less serious, problems for those attempting to adjust to the demands of an unfamiliar culture.

There is a growing recognition that the amount and depth of cross-cultural contact found the world over is likely to increase. Issues associated with this contact will gain increasing social importance. Growth in research—and in academic interest—in cross-cultural differences and contact between cultures is reflected in the increasing number and specializations of the academic journals on the subject (i.e., *International Journal of Intercultural Relations, International Migration Review.*) The importance of international trade and the strength of new players in the international business world (primarily Japan and the Pacific Rim countries) have led to unprecedented interest in international business and in the cultural differences in business practices (see Adler 1986). In today's world, as never before, the study of cross-cultural differences and the effect of cross-cultural contact have become an issue of considerable social interest and significance. As a result, a number of important applied psychological questions arise. What happens to people when they are thrown into an unfamiliar culture? What practices can make this experience easier and even enjoyable? What happens when two or more diverse cultural groups are forced to share the same location and resources? Some of the most relevant social issues of the 1990s involve questions of intercultural interaction, and an immediately practical application of both cross-cultural and social psychology is to aid in understanding—and perhaps improving—the quality of interactions among members of different cultures.

This chapter will discuss cross-cultural contact primarily at the individual level. However, the chapter ends with a brief discussion of cross-cultural contact at the collective or group level. At the individual level, we will discuss interpersonal contact, where an individual is faced with the challenge of coming to grips with life in a new and unfamiliar cultural milieu. This is the challenge faced by immigrants, refugees, foreign students, people working in foreign countries, and even travelers and tourists. At the collective level, we will discuss alternative strategies adopted by groups of people when they must share geographic space and resources with culturally diverse out-groups. This kind of large-scale, inter-group contact is best exemplified by large immigrant populations interacting with the majority population of their new home.

Interpersonal Cross-Cultural Contact

What are the processes and difficulties associated with adjusting to a new culture? What can be done to aid in the process and reduce the difficulties associated with moving into a new culture? Such questions have received considerable interest in the cross-cultural psychology literature. Cultural adjustment and acculturation, acculturative stress and culture shock, culture learning and cultural sensitivity are all well-developed themes. There are numerous books (e.g. Bochner 1981; Brislin 1981; Brislin et al. 1986; Casse 1980; Furnham and Bochner 1986; Harris and Moran 1979; Kohls 1981; Landis and Brislin 1983; Teagues 1976; Torbiorn 1982) and hundreds of chapters and journal articles providing descriptions of, and advice to improve, the adjustment of people who enter a culture unlike their own.

One consistent theme throughout this literature is that although it can be exciting, informative, and educational, adapting to a new culture is often a difficult, sometimes even destructive, experience. For nearly three decades, much of the research in cross-cultural contact has described the difficulties associated with entering and learning to live in a culture which is unfamiliar. In the next three sections, we will (1) describe the multifaceted nature of the process of cross-cultural adjustment, (2) present a model for describing the process of adjustment, (3) discuss several explanations for the difficulty of cross-cultural adjustment, and finally (4) discuss several predictors of the quality of adjustment.

Successful Cross-Cultural Interaction

Before we can discuss the predictors of the quality of adjustment to a new culture, it is necessary to define successful or effective adjustment and how cross-cultural psychologists study it. In addition, a further distinction needs to be made between adjustment to a new cultural environment, and enculturation (Taft 1977) or psychological acculturation (Berry 1990) into the host culture.

Adjustment

Adjustment is perhaps the most common general term used to describe the experience of learning to live in a new and different culture. The term "adjustment" has been used in a variety of ways in the literature on intercultural contact. There has also been some debate over what is involved in the "adjustment process" (see Bochner 1981; Furnham and Bochner 1986). Recent work indicates that the concept of cross-cultural adjustment is best viewed not as a unitary process, but as a multifaceted one (Armes and Ward 1989; Feinstein and Ward 1990; Grove and Torbiorn 1986; Searle and Ward 1990).

The first element might be referred to as psychological adjustment and is evaluated in terms of maintaining good mental health or psychological well-being. It is marked by a positive mood-state, feelings of contentment, and acceptance of one's new environment. This first component of adjustment is represented in the impression or feelings of the persons themselves. Persons experiencing successful psychological adjustment might say to themselves, "I feel comfortable here and I am generally happy to be here."

The second element of successful adjustment refers to the behavior of the individual. This type of adjustment has been called "culture-learning" (Bochner 1982) and involves the acquisition of appropriate social skills and behaviors to carry out successfully day-to-day activities. Several researchers propose a further division of this behavioral adjustment to distinguish between: (1) the development of social skills that allow for positive interpersonal relations with members of the host culture, and (2) demonstration of behaviors that result in effective accomplishment of one's required tasks (Hawes and Kealey 1981; Brislin et al. 1986).

Successful adjustment in terms of developing positive interpersonal relations would be demonstrated by someone spending time and sharing personal information with members of the host culture, by demonstrating respect for the new culture and its members, and by performing culturally appropriate behaviors necessary to gain the respect and liking of members of the host culture. In this case, successful adjustment would result in members of the host culture feeling that the newcomer fit in well and got along with others.

Determining successful adjustment in terms of task-effectiveness is, of course, dependent on the specific task required of the newcomer. In some cases, the required tasks of the newcomer are relatively clear and evaluation of their task-effectiveness is relatively easy. For students studying in a foreign university, we can simply look at their academic success. For the international salesperson attempting to open new overseas markets, we can simply look at his or her sales record. However, when the move to a new culture has no specific task-related purpose—as is the case of a refugee or immigrant—this element of adjustment would be determined by how effectively the person accomplishes everyday tasks. For example, how able was he or she to find a place to live, to find the means of supporting themselves and their dependents, and to acquire necessary services?

By the above description, successful cross-cultural adjustment would involve three elements; positive feelings and satisfaction with one's situation, the development of positive interpersonal relations with members of the host culture, and some level of effectiveness in carrying out the necessary tasks at hand. These three elements of adjustment are often closely related. Being accepted by the host society has been shown to be an important contributor to positive psychological adjustment

(Brislin 1981). In almost every context, success at one's tasks is likely to improve one's feelings of well-being and satisfaction (Abramson et al. 1978). Similarly, it is usually much easier to accomplish the required tasks if one is feeling good and has gained the acceptance and assistance of others (Furnham and Bochner 1982; Hammer 1987). Wendy Searle and Colleen Ward (1990), for example, have demonstrated the correlation between positive emotional states and task-effectiveness in an investigation involving adjustment of students from Malaysia and Singapore studying in New Zealand. The researchers found that measures of "psychological adjustment"—determined by low scores on a measure of depression—were the best predictors of task-effectiveness, measured in terms of the students' self-reported difficulty in carrying out activities of student life. These researchers also found that having satisfying interactions with members of the host culture was an important predictor of psychological adjustment.

The correlations of these three elements of adjustment is by no means perfect. Sojourners, for example, may feel fine and be enjoying their cross-cultural stay but may be ineffective in the task at hand (Kealey and Ruben 1983). Similarly, a person might be able to push ahead in accomplishing a task while being disliked by the hosts. In fact, in Searle and Ward's sample of South Asian students in New Zealand, only a small correlation was found between satisfactory relations with New Zealanders and effectiveness in day-to-day tasks. Thus, although there is likely to be some correlation between these three elements of adjustment, the strength of the correlation can vary between individuals and between contexts. For this reason, the three components must be evaluated separately in order to obtain a complete picture of an individual's adjustment to an unfamiliar culture.

Psychological Acculturation

Beyond simply adjusting to the demands of a new environment, long-term and permanent residents of a new culture may come to identify with the host culture. In this case, individuals are not simply able to function happily and effectively in the new culture; they actually become part of it. This "taking on" of a new cultural identity involves the integration of the values and beliefs of the culture into one's own understanding of the world. While an individual who has successfully adjusted to the new culture may understand and respect the attitudes, values, and beliefs of the new culture, the *acculturated* individual comes to hold these attitudes, beliefs, and values as his or her own. Similarly, a newcomer who has adjusted will know intellectually what behaviors are appropriate in the new culture, but the acculturated individual will act appropriately without thought or planning.

Ronald Taft (1977) describes an interesting analogy that may help to explain this distinction between successful adjustment and acculturation. A color-blind person learns to discriminate colors that in fact look the same to him or her, by picking out other characteristics that help to distinguish the colors. For example, he or she might learn the position of the green, yellow, and red lights on traffic signals. In this way, the color-blind individual may be fairly successful in dealing with a colorful world. This is the way a well-adjusted newcomer is successful in the new culture. However, the acculturated individual would be like an initially color-blind person who becomes able to actually see the colors and is able to actually experience the colorful world.

The process of psychological acculturation and true acceptance of a new culture usually requires a prolonged—or even permanent—stay in the new culture. It also requires intensive immersion in the new culture with little or no continued contact with one's native culture. In some cases, even these extreme pressures do not result in acculturation, and some individuals maintain a psychological distance from the new culture indefinitely.

Should psychological acculturation to the new culture occur, two alternative outcomes for the individual's original cultural identity are possible (Berry 1987). The individual's previous cultural identity can be replaced by the dominant culture in a process of subtractive culture learning (Lambert 1977; Taylor and Simard 1979). In this case, the individual essentially switches cultural identities. This process is consistent with the concept of assimilation, where the individual becomes a member of the new culture, while simultaneously losing his or her original cultural identity. This person may continue to understand and respect the original culture but no longer truly feels a part of that culture.

The alternative to assimilation is the integration of the new culture, while the original culture is maintained as a separate and distinct identity (Taft 1977). This process has been labeled "additive bi-culturalism" (Taylor 1991), and it is through this additive process that the individual can come to maintaining two separate cultural identities. This person is defined as truly bicultural if he or she is able to fully function as a member of either of the two cultural groups. Biculturalism can be understood as similar to bilingualism. The bilingual person speaks fluently and understands effortlessly both languages. Bilinguals are able, without conscious effort, to "plug in" to the appropriate language; their knowledge of a second language does not interfere with their ability to speak and understand the first.

There is clear evidence of the benefits of being bilingual (see Taylor 1991). However, the benefits of biculturalism have not yet been clearly established. Biculturalism may lead to greater flexibility in thinking, an enrichment of resources for coping, and increased understanding and tolerance of diversity and differences between oneself and others (Adler 1977; Brislin 1981). However, there is also the reasonable possibility that biculturalism may lead to identity conflict when the two cultural identities appear to be contradictory or in conflict (Adler 1975).

At present, there is little empirical evidence to support either of these positions and it is possible that there are both benefits and costs to biculturalism. However, research involving a variety of cultural groups both in Canada (e.g., O'Bryan et al. 1976; Taylor and Wright 1990) and the United States (e.g., Lambert and Taylor 1990), has shown that many immigrant and Native American groups, while motivated to acquire mainstream North American culture, are unwilling to abandon their heritage culture. These groups appear to be fighting against the pressures of subtractive biculturalism. For these groups the question of how to achieve additive biculturalism is of the utmost importance. Given the growing number, size, and militancy of groups determined to maintain their heritage culture, the question of how to promote and achieve biculturalism is likely to become one of the dominant educational and social questions in North America. In addition, the pressures of westernization and modernization felt by Third-World and Eastern European countries (see Moghaddam and Solliday 1991) make the possibility of biculturalism important in these parts of the world as well. The people of many nations are faced with the struggle between the desire to maintain their traditional ethnic identity and to embrace the modern world and its Western culture. Thus, the potential to achieve true biculturalism has ramifications worldwide. However, whatever the final outcome of intercultural interaction, there appears to be a relatively common pattern of adjustment that occurs when an individual first faces interaction with a novel culture. In the following section, we consider this initial adjustment process.

The Process of Cross-Cultural Adjustment

Intuitively, we might assume that the process of adjusting to life in a new culture follows a linear path, as illustrated in the left side of Figure 6.1. In this model, the individual learns more about life in the new culture and becomes increasingly adjusted to the new environment over time. However, research indicates that the path of adjustment to a new culture is more likely to follow the U-shaped curvilinear path shown in the right side of Figure 6.1 (Brein and David 1971; Deutsch and Won 1963; Gullahorn and Gullahorn 1963; Torbiorn 1982). After an initial stage of a fairly high level of adjustment to the new culture, the level declines and the person suffers a period of relatively poor adjustment. Then, usually, this period passes and gradually the individual achieves a higher and stable level of functioning in the new culture.

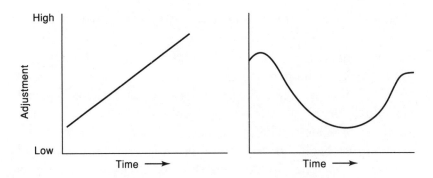

The adjustment of individuals to novel cultural surroundings over time.

The shape of the curve has been explained on the basis of the newcomer's emotional state during the adjustment period (Brislin 1981; Gullahorn and Gullahorn 1963). The high level of apparent adjustment demonstrated in the earliest stage results from the initial enthusiasm, anticipation, and novelty associated with entry into a new culture. Newcomers find an environment that is strange and involving. They have much to learn and many tasks to occupy their thoughts and their time. Although this early period can be stressful, the novelty and excitement of the early superficial contact with the new culture often results in a generally positive attitude and outward signs of successful adjustment.

As the novelty of the initial encounter begins to wane and the daily routine of existence in the new culture sets in, much of the romance of new experiences gives way to frustration and anxiety. A limited understanding of the native language and cultural habits makes interactions with members of the host culture demanding and tiresome. The newcomer may feel the effects of imagined or real discrimination by members of the host culture. The reality of the separation from the security of home and familiar traditions also becomes increasingly clear. All of these experiences lead to a decline in adjustment and a decrease in ability to cope with the demands of the new culture. The bottom of the U-shaped curve, when adjustment and mood are at their lowest, has been labeled "culture shock" (Oberg 1960). We will discuss the concept of culture shock in greater depth in a later section of this chapter. However, this particularly low point on the adjustment curve should be seen as a natural and likely outcome of immersion in a new environment.

With the passage of time and increased experience most individuals begin to learn—and sometimes even accept—the novel set of values, beliefs, and customs of their new environment. They begin to feel more positive and successful and develop competence in the new culture. Eventually, they may even come to view this new culture as truly their own.

The actual depth of the curve, the time associated with each stage in the process, the level of final adjustment, and a variety of other elements of this process can vary greatly from situation to situation and from individual to individual. Culture shock can affect the experienced traveler as profoundly as those on their first sojourn. In one context, a person may suffer the lowest point on the curve after only one or two months; in another environment, this point may be reached after many months or even years. Church (1982) points out that some sojourners may not start off in a state of optimism and excitement but may be unhappy or depressed right from the beginning of (or even before) their cross-cultural experience. The many potential variations in the actual shape of the curve have lead to some criticism of the U-shaped curve (Furnham and Bochner 1986) and it may be that the differences in adjustment pattern outweigh the similarities. However, the general pattern of adjustment described by the U-shaped curve can serve as a useful heuristic for understanding the process of adjustment to a new and unfamiliar culture.

The Difficulties of Cross-Cultural Interactions

The difficulties associated with immersion in a new and perhaps quite unfamiliar culture can result from a multitude of distinct causes. The four potential causes discussed in this section are:

stress, sense of loss, feelings of impotence, and ethnocentrism. Although this is by no means an exhaustive list, these four causes are often raised in discussion of culture shock and cultural adjustment (e.g., Adler 1986; Furnham and Bochner 1986; Taft 1977).

Stress Perhaps the simplest explanation for the difficulties associated with cross-cultural adjustment and the onset of culture shock is the stress associated with uncertainty and change (Guthrie 1975; Gudykunst and Hammer 1988). Anyone who has moved to a new city or town, or has left home to go to college, is familiar with the stress that goes with being uprooted, leaving friends and the security of familiar surroundings. We must make new friends, find a new home, and become familiar with a new environment. These new experiences are often exciting and interesting, but for most people they are also stressful. Consider then the level of stress associated with a move to a completely new culture, such as when an Asian, African, or Latin American immigrant or refugee arrives in North America, or when a Peace Corps worker is stationed in a village in Bangladesh. Not only do the newcomers have to make new friends, but their usual strategies for making friends may be completely inappropriate. Not only must they find a place to live but the accommodations available may be so unlike what they have known that their new "home" is incomprehensible and even frightening. Not only must they determine where to find the things that they need, they may not even know what things they might need. The people they must deal with are likely to dress differently, to have different work, eating, and social habits, and to speak a different language.

Sense of Loss Difficulties in cultural adjustment can also result from a sense of loss related to having been uprooted from one's original culture. One is suddenly deprived of friends and perhaps one's family, of one's status or position, perhaps of one's possessions. The person may feel the loss of familiar surroundings and miss the sense of feeling "at home." The intensity of this sense of loss and deprivation is likely to be mediated by the motivation for the move to the new culture. Feelings of loss are likely to be strongest for those forced to migrate, such as refugees, or someone transferred by a company, or the spouse and family of a diplomat or military officer. However, feelings of loss can be experienced to a lesser degree even by the most willing of voluntary settlers and sojourners.

Feelings of Impotence Perhaps the most commonly cited cause for the negative effect of immersion in an unfamiliar culture is the feelings of incompetence and inability to cope with the new environment. The newcomer may feel (often correctly) that he or she is unable to recognize what is appropriate behavior in a given context. Even simple tasks which were performed without thought or effort "back home" may now seem beyond one's capability.

The story of a friend of one of the authors (Stephen Wright) illustrates such feelings exactly. This young women was a refugee from Cambodia who arrived in Winnipeg, Canada, in the middle of January; a month when the average temperature is approximately 25 to 30 degrees (Celsius) below zero. Many months later, she described her first attempt to go grocery shopping in Winnipeg. Obtaining and preparing the family meal were tasks that she was highly competent at "back home" and ones that were basic to her role as a mother and head of the household.

> I first tried to prepare my 4-year-old daughter for the trip to the store. Although it was only down the street, the cold outside was beyond anything we had imagined. I put almost every piece of clothing we had in the house on to her and all I could on myself. You can imagine how we looked . . . Serin wearing three summer jackets and a man's hat and me in snowmobile boots and bare legs. The shopkeeper was very young and very unfriendly. I guess it was because of the way we were dressed, but how else were we to stay warm? The shop was only a small corner store and I could find nothing that I recognized except for the candy bars and the Coke. I

knew that would not do. My English was very bad, but I was able to get directions to a store where the shopkeeper said I would find much more food. The way he kept waving and pointing and his angry face made me feel very stupid and embarrassed that I had come into the wrong store. Lucky for us the other store was not too far. It turned out to be a huge Safeway. Imagine how I felt going into a Safeway. I had always shopped at an open market. Serin was frightened by all the people and the lights and noise and things. I felt terrible because I was as frightened as she was. We wandered around for a while and people stared at us. I couldn't tell what most of the things on the shelf were and of course I couldn't read any of the packages. We found the fresh vegetables and some of these I knew. We could not find meat and I was far too shy to ask anyone. But I did find a box with a chicken on the front. Although it seemed like a small box for chicken, we had been told that meat was very expensive in Canada. I followed people to the front to pay for the few things I had picked up. I was very afraid that I would not have enough money to pay for the things. . . . I really didn't know how much things cost. The beeping cash register and the moving table were amazing and frightening, and when the woman asked for my money, all I could do was hold out my hand full of bills and let her take what she wanted. The trip home was very cold and Serin was crying when we got home. I felt very bad for taking her out in the cold. As I began to prepare my meal, I soon found out that there was no chicken in the box with the chicken on it; only some powder with lots of salt in it, and some bags. I had bought "Shake 'n Bake" and had no meat at all. So the meal that I fed my family that night was several vegetables stirred in the "Shake 'n Bake" spices.

I can laugh a little when I talk about that day now. . . .but that was not a meal I was very proud of or that my family liked too much. Nobody complained, though. They could see the tears in my eyes when I served it.

As time passes, newcomers are likely to acquire some skills and knowledge of the new culture, and these gains may reduce the feelings of incompetence felt in the initial stages of the cross-cultural experience. However, these feelings of incompetence can reappear as newcomers begin to change their target of social comparison. Instead of comparing their own competence and success to that of other newcomers, they may begin now to make comparisons with members of the majority host culture. These new comparisons only serve to highlight again their relative social incompetence and can enhance other negative feelings and self-doubts.

Ethnocentrism Cross-cultural relocation, especially to a culture highly disparate from one's own, presents a large level of environmental change, which can lead to considerable uncertainty and difficulty in coping. However, environmental change in and of itself does not explain the difficulties usually associated with cross-cultural adjustment. As seen in the two previous causes, it is the psychological impact of these changes on the individual that are important. One of the major factors to determine psychological impact of a new environment on a given individual is his or her level of ethnocentrism (Church 1982). Ethnocentrism, in its most naive form, is the unquestioned assumption that one's own cultural values reflect objective reality. In this case, ethnocentric individuals fail even to recognize that another set of values and beliefs is possible. They blindly use their own set of values as the context for judging all objects and events. In its more complex form, ethnocentrism involves an awareness that there are other cultural perspectives, but these alternative views are judged to be inferior, incorrect, or immoral compared to one's own (Triandis 1990).

Some level of ethnocentrism is almost universal (LeVine and Campbell 1972). Virtually all cultural or national groups exhibit pride in, attachment to, and veneration for the symbols of their culture and its values. The vast majority of the members of a given cultural or national group will hold the symbols and habits of their own group in higher regard than the symbols and habits of others.

This tendency is easily understood when we consider that, from birth, we are socialized to accept a given set of norms defining a relatively narrow range of behaviors as appropriate and proper. Because the norms of behavior in one culture are often very different from those in another, a behavior that is inappropriate or taboo in one culture may be routine and quite appropriate in another. Our lifelong socialization in our own culture leaves us unprepared to deal with a different set of norms of behavior. When faced with contact with people from a different culture, we are likely to misunderstand or misinterpret their actions and words. For example, in Turkish culture, public physical contact such as embracing, walking hand-in-hand, and kissing on the cheek is commonly acceptable behavior between two heterosexual men. In North American culture, this type of contact has traditionally been perceived as "unmanly" and unacceptable. Although members of the homosexual community have done much to change North American norms concerning displays of public affection between men, many North American males might be offended if confronted with the "overly intimate" contact of a Turkish male.

Similarly, people from Nepal might be offended if you were to sit across from them with your feet outstretched. In Nepal, it is perceived as insulting to point the bottom of one's feet at someone. This norm also extends to shoes and, therefore, one should not place one's shoes so that the soles are pointing at someone or so that the soles are above someone's head. Even if aware of this cultural norm, a North American would likely find the Nepalese "preoccupation" with the bottom of the feet strange and even silly. Although she might attempt to obey the custom while in Nepal and avoided pointing the bottoms of her feet at others, it is unlikely that she would come to hold great respect for this custom or that she would now be offended should the bottoms of someone's feet happen to be pointed in her direction. Equally, it should be recognized that the uneasiness of many traditional North American males with a public embrace and kiss from another male would seem very strange and foolish to a Turk. It would take considerable experience for the Turk to completely appreciate the Americans' unease and much more before he would share that unease.

The strength of ethnocentrism can vary across cultures, as well as across time, situation, and individuals within a given culture. The small examples of cultural differences presented above, and our responses to them, show how difficult it would be to be completely absent of some level of ethnocentrism. For this reason, even when intercultural interactions are entered into with some level of sensitivity and a genuine interest in the other party's culture, some interactions can be difficult and troublesome. However, the more ethnocentric one's view, the more intolerant of other cultural groups one is likely to be—and this intolerance will lead to much more difficult intercultural interactions.

The other side of ethnocentrism is that of the host culture. Many host nations can be very ethnocentric in their treatment of newcomers from other cultures. For example, many North Americans have tended to believe that all arriving immigrants will want to discard the "primitive, old-fashioned" ways of their country of origin, and "become American" as quickly as they can. Ethnocentrism in Japan has resulted in a different response. Japanese culture has traditionally placed a high value on maintaining the purity of race. For this reason, Japan has tended to deny to non-Japanese entry and integration into Japanese society (Sethi 1975).

In many cases, the ethnocentric attitudes of the members of the host culture can result in prejudice and discrimination against the newcomers. This lack of respect for their cultural values and beliefs, and the resulting discrimination and rejection by the host, can be among the largest causes of adjustment problems for newcomers.

Of course, there is often an interaction between the newcomer's own ethnocentrism and the ethnocentrism of the host. A newcomer who demonstrates an attitude of superiority and fails to show sensitivity and respect for the host cultural norms is likely to elicit ethnocentric responses from members of the host culture. In this way, the newcomer's own ethnocentrism contributes to his or her own difficulties in adjustment. Alternatively, a newcomer who faces discrimination and disrespect at the hands of the dominant culture is likely to develop a negative attitude for the new culture and his or her own ethnocentric views will be hardened.

Ethnocentrism may not only have a negative effect on the adjustment of the newcomer, in some cases the ethnocentrism of the newcomer may result in damage to the host culture itself. This is typified by the cross-cultural contact of Western missionaries and Native peoples the world over. Although the intentions of the missionaries may have appeared admirable at the time, their ethnocentric view and their resulting efforts to "convert," "educate," and "civilize" native peoples demonstrates the worst kind of disregard and degradation of the native culture. In another example, North American tourists often demonstrate ethnocentrism in the attitudes they display towards the cultures of the countries they visit. Because of the financial benefits of tourism, many nations have erected whole communities and areas of their countries that reflect North American culture rather than their own. This self-effacing development has in many cases resulted in negative consequences for the people of these host nations (Pearce 1982). In the Pacific island of Tonga, for example, studies (Urbanowicz 1977, 1978) have shown that as a result of the large number of tourists who descend on the small port towns from cruise ships, many Tongan children beg rather than participate in traditional family activities or attend school. In addition, prostitution, drunkenness, and crime are also described as the direct result of the large scale tourist trade. The Seychelles Islands, promoted to tourists as the "islands of love" because of their traditionally uninhibited sexual standards, now have rampant and ferocious rates of venereal disease (Turner and Ash 1975). The selling of local culture to tourists has resulted in the trivializing of traditional events, ceremonies, and rituals as "quaint" and "cute" customs. In its worst form, this has resulted in the sacrilege of religious and cultural symbols through mass marketing of replicas (Crystal 1978; Mackenzie 1977). Finally, ethnocentrism is demonstrated by many multinational companies in their dealings with foreign governments, workers, and the physical environment. Many companies export products, such as chemicals and machinery, that are banned in their own nations. At some plants and factories in economically under-developed nations, workers are subjected to conditions well below those enjoyed by workers in the companies' country of origin. This exploitation represents an especially negative kind of ethnocentrism on the part of economically advantaged nations.

Variables That Can Aid or Disrupt Adjustment

Several variables that might contribute to the level of difficulty in adjustment have been mentioned, such as the motivation for entering the new culture, and discrimination by members of the host culture. A variety of other specific variables that seem to affect successful adjustment to a new cultural environment have been identified.

Divergence of New Culture from One's Own The disparity between one's own culture and the host culture affects how severe will be the uncertainty and change (see Furnham and Bochner 1982). Obviously, a North American student who goes to England to study is likely to face substantially fewer disruptive life changes, and would be less likely to feel incompetent, than if she was to study in Nigeria or Japan. Interestingly, however, research has shown that it may not always be the actual difference between the two cultures that determines adjustment difficulties. Instead, it is the individual's perceptions of how distant the home culture is from the host culture (Searle and Ward 1990). Thus, two members of the Peace Corps who are both stationed in the same village in Morocco may suffer different levels of difficulty adjusting. The cause may be that one looks for and finds the similarities between Moroccan and American culture, while the other attends to the differences.

Social Support The value of support gained from interpersonal relations with others in easing adjustment may appear obvious. However, who the interpersonal relationship is with and the type of support provided can be important. Research has found that assistance from, and close relationships with, members of the host culture is associated with improved cross-cultural adjustment (Benson 1978; Richardson 1974). Even a single close friend who is a host member can result in fewer difficulties for the newcomer (Sellitiz and Cook 1962). These intercultural friendships appear to be an essential ingredient in the learning of social skills in the new society (Furnham and Bochner 1982). These relationships can also "open doors" for the pursuit of such desired goals as employment and membership in desired social groups (Kim 1978; Pruitt 1978). Unfortunately, there is evidence to show that close friendships between newcomers and host nationals may be difficult to form (Furnham and Bochner 1982, 1986). Ethnocentrism and uneasiness on both sides lead many newcomers to avoid intimate contact with hosts.

There is also evidence that social support gained from relationships with one's own culture can be beneficial in the adjustment process of immigrants (Kim 1978) and Peace Corps workers (Arnold 1967). Association with a familiar and accepting group may reduce the pressures of adjustment (Taft 1977). However, interaction with other newcomers does not always have a positive impact on adjustment (Berry and Blondel 1982; Berry et al. 1987; Pruitt 1978). Research has pointed out that association with others who are also struggling with the stresses of adjustment may result in the "contagion effect." This effect refers to how one stressed individual can "infect" others vulnerable to similar stress. Sharing personal "disaster stories" and romanticizing about home-sweet-home can serve to exacerbate frustrations with the new environment and feelings of homesickness. Commiseration among compatriots experiencing the stress of cross-cultural adjustment can result in "a sinking-ship morale," which further reduces the ability of each person to cope (Adelman 1988). Similarly, Richard Brislin (1981) points out that having one's spouse or family along can often exacerbate cultural adjustment problems rather than reduce them:

> One's spouse has to establish interpersonal relations since the couple is rarely together throughout the entire day. If there are children they will want to play with others their own

age. . . . even the most successful marriages may attempt a
catharsis by unloading their feelings on each other. The
result may be an escalation of tension. (109)

The presence of a substantial compatriot community can
also reduce the individual's integration into the new culture by
allowing the person to isolate him- or herself from the host
culture. This is particularly apparent in the case of overseas military placements. Military personnel are often isolated from the
cultures in which they are stationed. They are given little opportunity for real interaction with the host culture. Thus, their ethnocentric views go untested, and their limited interactions with
"the locals" often reflect these ethnocentric biases. These individuals are likely to show little adjustment to the new culture
and are likely to gain little from the cross-cultural experience.

It appears that there are three variables that impact on
whether interaction and interpersonal relations with other newcomers will assist or hinder adjustment. First, a social network of
conationals that prevents the development of close relations with
members of the host culture is likely to slow or prevent adjustment to the new culture. Second, strong relationships with members of one's native culture seem to have a less detrimental effect
on adjustment when the cross-cultural contact is long-term (as in
the case of immigration) rather than short-term (as in the case of
foreign students, business persons, and tourists). Finally, the content of the interaction with conationals is important. Arnold
(1967) found that when groups of Peace Corps workers got together and praised each other's projects, tried to lift each other's
spirits, or suggested means of achieving goals, the interactions
improved later adjustment.

Personality There has been considerable effort to try to uncover
a set of personality characteristics that lead to success in cross-
cultural interactions. Several attempts have been made to
describe the "universal communicator" (Gardner 1962), or the
"multicultural personality" (Adler 1974) or the "universal person" (Walsh 1973). These descriptions of a specific personality

optimal for cross-cultural interaction have not held up well to empirical research (Van den Broucke et al. 1989; Stenning 1979).

Two interesting alternatives to the idea of specific cross-cultural personality type have been presented. First, it may be that it is specific behaviors rather than personality characteristics that distinguish those that seem to adjust more rapidly and effectively to new cultural situations. Researchers have identified specific communication skills, several specific behavioral strategies for interacting with others, and a number of specific coping behaviors that have been associated with successful adjustment among sojourners (Hammer 1987).

Emphasis on behaviors, rather than personality, has some interesting implications. If success in cross-cultural experiences is dependent on personality, there is little that can be done to improve a given individual's likelihood of success in a new culture. In this case, the emphasis would be on selection of the right type of person when cross-cultural experiences are planned, such as the Peace Corps, international student exchanges, or overseas business representatives. Alternatively, if the cross-cultural experience was unplanned, as in the case of a refugee or immigrant, the emphasis would be on distinguishing those who are at the greatest risk and providing them with support and assistance. The emphasis on behaviors, however, implies that the skills necessary for successful cross-cultural contact can be learned and, therefore, taught.

The second interesting finding of the question of a cross-cultural personality involves the idea of "cultural fit" in interpersonal interaction style (Searle and Ward 1990). The notion of a "cultural fit" predicts that the more closely the individual's personality traits match the social norms of the host culture, the more easily they will adjust to the new culture. This concept provided an explanation for some perplexing research findings. It was found that among Chinese students studying at New Zealand universities, the more extroverted the students, the better their psychological adjustment to New Zealand culture. This finding was inconsistent with previous research with a group of

Western expatriates in Singapore (Armes and Ward 1989) that had shown that being more extroverted resulted in poorer adjustment. Taken together, it at first appears that these two studies indicate that extroversion is not a good predictor of adjustment to a new culture. However, the contradiction can be explained by the idea of "cultural fit." The personality trait of extroversion interacts with the specific characteristics of a given culture to predict psychological adjustment. Chinese culture discourages behaviors consistent with extroversion far more than do Western such cultures as the dominant culture of New Zealand (Eysenck and Long 1986). Therefore, extroverted Westerners are more likely than their more introverted conationals to act in a manner inconsistent with Chinese culture. Similarly, Western culture tends to encourage behaviors consistent with extroversion; thus, the most extroverted of the Chinese sojourners might be most likely to exhibit behaviors consistent with New Zealand culture. Therefore, the individuals who more easily exhibit culturally relevant behaviors will more easily adjust to the new host culture.

Expectations Several researchers have uncovered findings related to the prior expectations of the newcomer and their subsequent adjustment. These findings vary somewhat concerning the precise nature of the relationship between expectations and adjustment. Some seem to support a direct relationship between expectations and adjustment, in that those who expect the worst have the most difficulties (Searle and Ward 1990). Other findings seem to support the view that expectations that include some knowledge about culture shock and possible problems with adjustment will be beneficial (Locke and Feinsod 1982; Wiessman and Furnham 1987). However, what appears to be the most important element is that expectations be in line with what one is likely to experience. For example, research with the Peace Corps has found that workers who are placed in cultural contexts most divergent from their home culture were often more satisfied, more enthusiastic, more effective, and less likely to terminate their stays early than were workers who were placed in more Westernized cultural contexts (Jones and Popper 1972).

This was an unexpected and counter-intuitive finding. The explanation appears to be in the worker's expectations. Peace Corps workers generally expected to be seen by host country nationals as unusual, as outsiders who could provide something unavailable. In more remote settings, where previous contact with other foreigners was limited, the worker was most likely to be perceived in this manner. In more economically developed locations, the role of the workers was much less innovative and they were at times seen by host nationals as "just another foreigner doing what others had done before." In such situations, although the cultural context was much closer to the home culture of the Peace Corps workers, it did not match their expectations. This disappointment resulted in their attitudes, performance, and level of satisfaction being consistently poorer than those whose expectations were consistent with what they experienced. It appears that if the new cultural experience is inconsistent with one's expectations, adjustment can be much more difficult (Taft 1977).

Findings that point to the importance of realistic expectations have implications for the overly optimistic expectations of many immigrants concerning what life in America will be like. The "streets of gold/world of opportunity" view common among immigrants and refugees anticipating a move to America, can be an important contributor to their difficult adjustment. In fact, Cochrane (1983) believes that positive expectations on the part of immigrants from economically developing nations is inversely related to adjustment.

Of course, there are many other specific variables that contribute to the speed and difficulties experienced during cross-cultural adjustment. In addition, these variables may interact with one another to determine the overall success of final adjustment. Finally, different variables may contribute differentially to the different types of cultural adjustment discussed earlier. Much more research must be done to untangle completely the relationship between situational conditions, the characteristics and skills of individuals, and their long-term and short-term adjustment to a new culture. However, this research will continue to assist those interested in the training and support of sojourners and migrants to a new culture, as well as those offering support and education to immigrants and refugees attempting to come to grips with adjustment to their new cultural surroundings. The questions of cultural adjustment, acculturation, and biculturalism are likely to become increasingly important as technological and social change truly make our planet a global village.

Intergroup Cross-Cultural Contact: Multiculturalism or Assimilation

From the point of view of the United States, the predominant social psychological theme at the group level has revolved around race relations. Indeed, one observer has described "America" in terms of three national preoccupations; war and peace, bread and butter, and black and white (cited in Lambert and Taylor 1990). Wallace Lambert and Donald Taylor (1990) have argued that challenging the preoccupation with black and white is a more broadly based concern for race, culture, and language in the context of immigration. At the heart of this preoccupation is a fundamental concern for what is "American" and what is "un-American."

This preoccupation with what is and what isn't "American" places intergroup cross-cultural contact squarely in focus. Moreover, it offers another dramatic instance where cross-cultural research has brought new perspectives to bear on what many would argue is the most emotionally loaded issue in America, and indeed the whole world—how a society can cope with racial and cultural diversity.

The historic American approach to this issue is captured in the romantic image of the melting pot (described at the beginning of this chapter). Essentially, the idea is that cultural minorities should abandon or toss aside their "old ways," their heritage culture, and adopt the "American way." If enough heat could be applied to the pot, cultural differences would "melt" away and everyone would be culturally the same—"American." This political philosophy of assimilation is completely consistent with theory in social psychology linking similarity and attraction (Byrne 1971). Two decades of social psychological research indicates that the more similar two people are in terms of attitudes, activities, beliefs and—of significance for the present context—ethnic group, the more they will like each other (Kandel 1978; Simard 1981). The social psychological rationale for the melting pot or assimilation ideology, then, is that if racial and cultural groups give up their heritage culture, a culturally homogeneous society will arise, wherein interpersonal attraction will be based on individual similarities and not on cultural characteristics. The end result would be a society that escapes the stresses of racial and cultural conflict.

The melting pot or assimilationist ideology is rooted in political and social psychological theory that originates in the United States. Most nations of the world are multiracial and multiethnic, and thus racial and cultural diversity are taken for granted. For example, in Canada the basic political philosophy is that the nation is comprised of two founding groups—French and English. Beyond this dualism, other cultural groups are encouraged to retain their heritage culture as much as possible. This policy of multiculturalism was introduced formally in 1971 and has led to a new set of images including the mosaic, tossed salad, and patchwork quilt as replacements for the American melting pot.

The underlying social psychological rationale for the multicultural position is that only when members of a cultural group feel secure in their own identity can they feel open and charitable toward other cultural groups. Interestingly, the most influential social psychological theorizing consistent with this theme is social identity theory—a theory whose originators were European social psychologists. Social identity theorists argue that people strive to belong to groups that are distinct and that are positively valued. Thus, in direct opposition to the U.S.-based similarity/attraction relationship, social identity theory would propose that if a cultural group was stripped of its uniqueness, it would feel threatened and insecure. This insecurity would result in intergroup strife, as the threatened group attempted to reestablish its uniqueness.

The decision of which of these two perspectives (assimilation or multiculturalism) to support has important implications for a given society. For example, if an assimilationist approach is adopted, the role of the education system—and schools in particular—would be to teach the majority culture and language to newcomers as quickly as possible. However, under a policy of multiculturalism, classrooms would recognize and encourage cultural differences in learning style, attitudes, and values. Heritage languages would be taught in school. This difference in orientation might also be reflected in the economic, legal, even political arenas. Thus, the decision to support an assimilationist or multicultural approach to intercultural relations would likely have a direct impact on every member of the society.

There remains considerable debate concerning the merits of these two competing views of how to approach intercultural contact at the intergroup level (e.g., Berry 1984; Frideres 1989; Lambert and Taylor 1990; Pettigrew 1988; Taylor 1991). Many of the same trends that have resulted in increased cross-cultural contact at the interpersonal level, described at the outset of this chapter, are also increasing the amount of contact at intergroup level. It is, therefore, likely that the debate over the relative merits of assimilation versus multiculturalism will continue to grow in intensity and that this area will attract increasing theoretical and empirical examination.

Conclusion

Formerly, the study of cross-cultural contact attracted little scientific interest. With little real contact between culturally divergent groups, this area was of little general concern. Similarly, cross-cultural psychology has traditionally been of little real interest to most of the rest of social psychology (Amir and Sharon 1987;

Tedeschi 1988; Wheeler and Reis 1988). Except for the few social psychologists working in other parts of the world, there was little real need for concern about how people in other places around the globe behaved (Moghaddam 1987; Bond 1988). However, just as the increase in contact between culturally divergent groups has resulted in a growing need to understand the process and outcome of intercultural contact, demographic and social changes have made apparent the need to incorporate cross-cultural concerns into the mainstream of social psychology. It appears that there are some interesting parallels between the increasing importance of research on cross-cultural contact and the introduction of a cross-cultural perspective in social psychology.

It is, therefore, appropriate that we conclude this chapter and this book with a discussion of the benefits of cross-cultural contact. Many of the benefits gained by individuals who experience positive contact with people from a different culture seem to mirror the benefits gained by the student of social psychology who adopts a cross-cultural perspective.

In the opening chapter, and throughout this text, we have pointed out that many of the findings of social psychology may not generalize across cultures. We have proposed that the adoption of a cross-cultural perspective might lead social psychologists, at very least, to recognize the limitations of their findings. By becoming aware of the considerable differences between one's own culture and others, the social psychologist is made aware that what he or she thought to be a principle of human behavior may not hold in cultures other than his or her own. A very similar realization has been documented for those who have experienced cross-cultural contact. Research has shown that intercultural experiences can lead to increased cultural awareness and a more culturally cosmopolitan outlook (Carson and Widaman 1985; Kâgitçibasi 1978; Sharma and Jung 1985). Meaningful and extended interaction with members of other cultures leads subjects to greater recognition that one's own values are not universal and that the values of other societies may be just as valid.

We have also suggested that a cross-cultural perspective will broaden the scope and nature of the issues and problems that social psychology will consider. Social psychology has described much that is of great interest. However, in this text, we have, at times, echoed the question asked by a past editor of the *Journal of Cross-Cultural Psychology*, Roy Malpass: "Is the knowledge we have attained available because it is more important than the knowledge we did not get, or is it present simply because a few people worked on these rather than other questions?" (1988, 33). One way to answer this question is to broaden the nature of our investigations through the adoption of a cross-cultural perspective. Testing and expanding the limits of one's knowledge has also been described as one of the positive outcomes of successful intercultural experiences (Paige 1990). For example, high levels of interpersonal interaction with international students results in more elaborate career aspirations for American college students (Sharma and Jung 1985).

There is also evidence that cross-cultural contact leads to greater interest in people and information from other cultures (Paige 1990). Individuals who have themselves spent time in another country tend to be more interested in interacting with and befriending people from other cultures (Furnham and Bochner 1986). Those who have had intercultural experiences also report greater interest in international and multicultural issues (Carson and Widaman 1985; Flack 1976; Klineberg 1981). Similarly, it is our belief that the adoption of a cross-cultural perspective will lead social psychology to be more aware of and receptive to the theories, research, and methodologies being developed in other parts of the world.

Finally, we have argued often in this book that a cross-cultural perspective will offer students of social psychology a greater understanding, not only of other cultures, but of their own culture as well. Equivalently, individual contact with other cultures has been shown to increase a participant's respect, understanding, and awareness of his or her own culture (Klineberg and Hull 1979; Sharma and Jung 1985; Steinkalk and Taft 1979). For example, Jerry Carson and Keith Widaman (1985) provide evidence that a sojourn abroad results in more mature and objective perceptions of one's home country.

In this chapter, we have discussed the challenges that may face an individual or a society attempting to adjust and adapt to cultural diversity. Despite the obstacles and potential difficulties, it appears that cross-cultural contact can have very important benefits for those who meet the challenge. It is our hope that this book has assisted the student of social psychology in a similar challenge. Despite the potential obstacles, there is a growing sense that the time has come for social psychology to recognize the important potential contributions of cross-cultural psychology. We hope that the cross-cultural perspective described in this text will contribute to this bridge-building process.

References

Abramson, L. Y., Seligman, M. E. P., and Teasdale, J. D. (1978). Learned helplessness in humans: Critique and reformulation, *Journal of Personality and Social Psychology, 87,* 49–74.

Adair, J. (1989). *Indigenous Developments in Indian Psychology: A Quantitative Assessment.* Paper presented at the Canadian Psychological Association meeting, Halifax.

Adair, G., Dushenko, T. W., and Lindsay, R. C. L. (1985). Ethical regulations and their impact on research practice. *American Psychologist, 40,* 59–72.

Adelman, M. B. (1988). Cross-cultural adjustment: A theoretical perspective on social support, *International Journal of Intercultural Relations, 12,* 183–204.

Adler, N. J. (1986). *International Dimensions of Organizational Behavior.* Boston: Kent.

Adler, P. S. (1974). Beyond cultural identity: Reflections upon cultural and multicultural man. *Topics in Cultural Learning, 2,* 23–41.

Adler, P. S. (1975). The transitional experience: An alternative view of culture shock. *Journal of Humanistic Psychology, 15,* 13–23.

Adler, P. S. (1977). Beyond cultural identity: Reflections upon cultural and multicultural man. In R. W. Brislin (ed.), *Culture Learning: Concepts, Applications, and Research.* Honolulu: University Press of Hawaii.

Adorno, T. W., E. Frenkel-Brunswik, D. J. Levinson, and B. W. Sanford (1950). *The Authoritarian Personality.* New York: Harper & Row.

Agnihotri, R. (April 1990). Personal communication.

Aiello, J. B. (1987). Human spacial behavior. In D. Stokols and I. Altman (eds.), *Handbook of Environmental Psychology.* vol.1, 505–531. New York: Wiley-Interscience.

Ajzen, I. 1988. *Attitudes, Personality and Behavior.* Chicago, Ill.: Dorsey Press.

Alcock, J. E., Carment D. W., and Sadava, S. W. (1988). *A Textbook of Social Psychology.* Scarborough, Canada: Prentice-Hall.

Almond G. A., and Verba, S. (1963). *The Civic Culture.* Princeton N.J.: Princeton University Press.

Amir, Y., and Sharon, I. (1987). Are social-psychological laws cross-culturally valid? *Journal of Cross-Cultural Psychology, 18,* 383–470.

Ancona, L., and Pareyson, R. (1968). Contributo allo studie della agressione: la dinamica della obbedienza distruttiva. *Archivadi psicologia neurologia e psichiatria, 29,* 340–372.

Argyle, M. (1982). Inter-cultural communication. In S. Bochner (ed.), *Cultures in Contact: Studies in Cross-Cultural Interaction.* Oxford: Pergamon.

Argyle, M. (1988). A social psychologist visits Japan. *The Psychologist, 1,* 361–363.

Argyle, M. (1988). Social relations. In M. Hewstone, W. Stroebe, J. Codol, and G. M. Stephenson (eds.), *Introduction to Social Psychology: A European Perspective.* Oxford: Basil Blackwell.

Argyle, M., and Furnham, A. (1983). Sources of satisfaction and conflict in long-term relationships. *Journal of Marriage and the Family, 45,* 481–493.

Argyle, M., and Henderson, M. (1985). *The Anatomy of Relationships: And the Rules and Skills Needed to Manage Them Successfully.* London: Heinemann.

Argyle, M., Henderson, M., and Furnham, A. (1985). The rules of social relationships. *British Journal of Social Psychology, 24,* 125–139.

Argyle, M., Henderson, M., Bond, M. H., Iizuka, Y., and Contarello, A. (1986). Cross-cultural variations in relationship rules. *International Journal of Psychology, 21,* 287–315.

Armes, K., and Ward, C. (1989). Cross-cultural transitions and sojourner adjustment in Singapore. *Journal of Social Psychology, 129,* 273–275.

Arnold, C. (1967). Culture shock in a Peace Corps field mental health program. *Community Mental Health Journal, 3,* 53–60.

Arnold, M. (1969). *Culture and Anarchy.* Cambridge: Cambridge University Press.

Aronson, E., Brewer, M. B., and Carlsmith, J. M. (1985). Experimentation in social psychology. In G. Lindzey and E. Aronson (eds.), *Handbook of Social Psychology*, 441–486. New York: Random House.

Aronson, E., Ellsworth, P. C., Carlsmith, J. M, and Gonzales, M. H. (1990). *Methods of Research in Social Psychology*. 2d. ed.New York: McGraw-Hill.

Asch, S. E. (1956). Studies of conformity and independence: A minority of one against a unanimous majority. *Psychological Monographs, 70* (9, whole no. 416).

Austin, W. G., and Worshel, S. (1979). *The Social Psychology of Intergroup Relations.* Monterey, Calif.: Brook/Cole.

Bacon, M. K., Child, I. L., and Barry, H., III. (1963). A cross-cultural study of correlates of crime. *Journal of Abnormal and Social Psychology, 66,* 291–300.

Bandura, A. (1973). *Aggression: A Social Learning Analysis.* Englewood Cliffs, N.J.: Prentice-Hall, Inc.

Bandura, A., and Walters, R. (1963). *Social Learning and Personality Development.* New York: Holt, Rinehart and Winston.

Baron, R. A. (1977). *Human Aggression.* New York: Plenum.

Barry, H., Child, I., and Bacon, M. (1959). Relationship of child training to subsistence economy. *American Anthropologist, 61,* 51–63.

Barry, H., III, Josephson, L., Lauer, E., and Marshall, C. (1976). Traits enculcated in childhood: Cross-cultural codes V. *Ethnology, 15,* 83–114.

Baumrind, D. (1964). Some thought on ethics of research: After reading Milgram's "Behavioral study of obedience." *American Psychologist, 19,* 421–423.

Befu, H. (1971). *Japan: An Anthropological Introduction.* San Francisco: Chandler.

Bellak, L., and Antell, M. (1974). An intercultural study of aggressive behavior on children's playgrounds. *American Journal of Orthopsychiatry, 44,* 503–511.

Bellak, L. (1990). Why I fear the Germans. *New York Times,* April 25.

Bem, S. L. (1974). The measurement of psychological androgyny. *Journal of Consulting and Clinical Psychology, 42,* 155–162.

Bem, S. L. (1984). Androgyny and gender schema theory: A conceptualization and empirical integration. In R. A. Dienstbier (ed.), *Nebraska Symposium on Motivation,* 179–226. Lincoln: University of Nebraska Press.

Benson, P. (1978). Measuring cross-cultural adjustment: The problem of criteria. *International Journal of Intercultural Relations, 2,* 21–37.

Berlyne, D. E. (1968). American and European psychology. *American Psychologist, 23,* 447–452.

Berman, J. J., Murphy-Berman V., and Singh, P. (1985). Cross-cultural similarities and differences in perceptions of fairness. *Journal of Cross-Cultural Psychology, 16,* 55–67.

Berry, J. W. (1966). Temne and Eskimo perceptual skills. *International Journal of Psychology, 1,* 207–229.

Berry, J. W. (1967). Independence and conformity in subsistence-level societies. *Journal of Personality and Social Psychology, 7,* 415–418.

Berry, J. W. 1970. A functional approach to the relationship. between stereotypes and familiarity. *Australian Journal of Psychology, 22,* 29–33.

Berry, J. W. (1976). *Human Ecology and Cognitive Style: Comparative Studies in Cultural and Psychological Adaptation.* New York: Sage/Halsted/Wiley.

Berry, J. W. (1984). Cultural relations in plural societies: Alternatives to segregation and their sociopsychological implications. In N. Miller and M. B. Brewer (Eds.), *Groups in Contact: The Psychology of Desegregation.* Orlando, Fla.: Academic Press.

Berry, J. W. (1987). Finding identity: Separation, integration, assimilation, or marginality? In L. Driedger (ed.), *Ethnic Canada: Identities and Inequalities.* Toronto: Copp Clark Pitman.

Berry, J. W. (1990). Psychology of acculturation: Understanding individuals moving between cultures. In R. W. Brislin (ed.), *Applied Cross-Cultural Psychology.* Newbury Park Calif.: Sage.

Berry, J. W., Kim, U., Minde, T., and Mok, D. (1987). Comparative studies of acculturative stress. *International Migration Review, 21,* 490–511.

Blake, R. R., Shepard, H. A., and Mouton, J. S. (1964). *Managing Intergroup Conflict in Industry.* Houston: Gulf.

Bochner, S. (1982). The social psychology of cross-cultural relations. In S. Bochner (ed.), *Cultures in Contact: Studies in Cross-Cultural Interaction.* Oxford: Pergamon Press.

Bochner, S., ed. (1981). *The Mediating Person: Bridges Between Cultures.* Boston: G. K. Hall.

Bond, M. 1983. A proposal for cross-cultural studies of attribution. In M. Hewstone, (Ed.). *Attribution theory: Social and functional extensions.* pp. 144–157. Oxford: Basil Blackwell.

Bond, M. H. (1988). *The Cross-Cultural Challenge to Social Psychology.* Newbury Park, Calif.: Sage.

Bond, M. H. (1988). Introduction. In M. H. Bond (ed.) *The Cross-Cultural Challenge to Social Psychology.* Newbury Park, Calif.: Sage.

Brein, M., and David, K. H. (1971). Intercultural communications and the adjustment of the sojourner. *Psychological Bulletin, 76,* 216–230.

Briggs, J. L. (1971). Kapluna daughter: Adopted by the Eskimo. In J. P. Spradley and D. W. McCurdy (eds.), *Conformity and Conflict: Readings in Cultural Anthropology,* 61–79. Boston: Little Brown.

Brigham, J. C. (1971). Ethnic stereotypes. *Psychological Bulletin, 76,* 15–38.

Brislin, R. W. (1981). *Cross-Cultural Encounter: Face-to-Face Interaction.* New York: Pergamon Press.

Brislin, R. W., Cushner, K., Cherrie, C., and Yong, M. (1986). *Intercultural Interaction: A Practical Guide.* Newbury Park, Calif.: Sage.

Bronfenbrenner, U. (1970). *Two Worlds of Childhood: U.S. and U.S.S.R.* New York: Russell Sage Foundation.

Brown, Roger. (1966). *Social Psychology.* New York: The Free Press.

Brown, Roger. (1986) *Social Psychology: The Second Edition.* New York: The Free Press.

Brown, Rupert. (1988). *Group Process: Dynamics Within and Between Groups.* Oxford: Basil Blackwell.

Byrne, D. (1969). Attitudes and attraction. In L.Berkowitz (ed.), *Advances in Experimental Social Psychology.* vol. 4. New York: Academic Press.

Byrne, D. (1971). *The Attraction Paradigm.* New York: Academic Press.

Carlson M., and Miller, N. (1988). Bad experiences and aggression. *SSR, 72,* 155–157.

Carson, J. S., and Widaman, K. F. (1985). The effects of study abroad during college on attitudes towards other cultures. *International Journal of Intercultural Relations, 12,* 1–17.

Casse, P. (1980). *Training the Cross-Cultural Mind: A Handbook for Cross-Cultural Trainers and Consultants.* Washington, D.C.: SIETAR.

Castro, M. A. C. (1974). Reactions to receiving aid as a function of cost to donor and opportunity to aid. *Journal of Applied Social Psychology, 4,* 194–209.

Chagnon, N. A. (1974). *Studying the Yanomano.* New York: Holt, Rinehart and Winston.

Chandler, T., Shama, D. A., Wolf, F. M., and Planshard, S. K. (1981). Multi-attributional causality for achievement across five cross-national samples. *Journal of Cross-cultural Psychology, 12,* 207–221.

Chandra, S. (1973). The effects of group pressure on perception: a cross-cultural conformity study. *International Journal of Psychology, 8,* 37–39.

Chatterjee, B. B. (1975). Training and preparation for research in intercultural relations in the Indian subcontinent. In D. Landis and R. W. Brislin (eds.), *Handbook of Intercultural Training. Vol. 3: Area Studies in Intercultural Training.* New York: Pergamon Press.

Christie, R. (1965). Some implications of research trends in social psychology. In O. Klineberg and R. Christie (eds.), *Perspectives in Social Psychology* 141–152. New York: Holt, Rinehart and Winston.

Church, A. T. (1982). Sojourner adjustment. *Psychological Bulletin, 91,* 540–572.

Civcivelli, B. G. (1980). Social services and the kin network: View of the elderly. *Journal of Home Economics, 3,* 34–37.

Claeys, W. (1967). Conforming behavior and personality variables in Congolese students. *International Journal of Psychology, 2,* 13–23.

Clark, M. S., Gotay, G. C., and Mills, J. (1974). Acceptance of help as a function of the potential helper and opportunity to repay. *Journal of Applied Social Psychology, 4,* 224–229.

Cochrane, R. (1983). *The Social Creation of Mental Illness.* London: Longman.

Cousins, S. (1989). Culture and self-perception in Japan and in the United States. *Journal of Personality and Social Psychology, 56,* 124–131.

Crocker, J., and Major, B. (1989). Social stigma and self-esteem: The self-protective properties of stigma. *Psychological Review, 96,* 608–630.

Crystal, E. (1978). Tourists in Toraja, Sulawesi, and Indonesia. In V. Smith (Ed.), *Hosts and Guests.* Oxford: Blackwell.

Daley, M., and Wilson, M. (1988). *Homicide.* New York: Aldine de Gruyter.

Darwin, C. (1859). *On the Origin of Species by Means of Natural Selection, or the Preservation of Favoured Races in the Struggle for Life.* London: John Murray.

Davidson, A. R., and Thompson, E. 1980. Cross-cultural studies of attitudes and beliefs. In H. C. Triandis and R. N. Brislin (eds.) *Handbook of Cross-Cultural Psychology.* vol. 5, 25-71. Boston: Allyn and Bacon.

Deal, T. E., and Kennedy, A. A. (1982). *Corporate Cultures: The Rites and Rituals of Corporate Life.* Reading, Mass.: Addison-Wesley.

Deutsch, M. (1975). Equity, equality, and need: What determines which value will be used as the basis of distributive justice? *Journal of Social Issues, 31,* 137–149.

Deutsch, S. E., and Won, G. Y. M. (1963). Some factors in the adjustment of foreign national in the United States. *Journal of Social Issues, 19,* 115–122.

Diab, L. N. (1970). A study of intragroup and intergroup relations among experimentally produced groups. *Genetic Psychology Monographs, 82,* 49–82.

Doise, W. (1978). *Groups and Individuals: Explanations in Social Psychology.* Cambridge: Cambridge University Press.

Dovidio, J. F., and Gaertner, S. L., eds. (1986). *Prejudice, Discrimination, and Racism.* London: Academic Press.

Doyle, J. A., and Paludi, M. A. (1991). *Sex and Gender: The Human Experience.* 2d. ed. New York: W. C. Brown.

Eisenberg, N., and Lennon, R. (1983). Sex differences in empathy and related capacities. *Psychological Bulletin, 94,* 100–131.

Eldersveld, S. J., and Dodge, R. W., 1954. Personal contact or mail propaganda? An experiment in voting turnout and attitude change. In D. Katz, D. Cartwright, S. Eldersveld, and A. M. Lee (eds.), *Public Opinion and Propaganda.* New York: Dryden Press.

Elms, A. C., and Milgram, S. (1966). Personality characteristics associated with obedience and defiance toward authoritarian command. *Journal of Experimental Research in Personality, 1,* 282-289.

Ember, C. R. (1981). A cross-cultural perspective on sex differences. In R. H. Munroe, R. L. Munroe & B. B. Whiting (eds.), *Handbook of Cross-Cultural Human Development,* 531-580. New York: Garland.

Ember, C. R., and Ember, M. (1985). *Anthropology*. 4th ed. Englewood Cliffs, NJ.: Prentice-Hall.

Emswiller T., Deaux, K., and Willits, J. E. (1971). Similarity, sex and requests for small favors. *Journal of Applied Social Psychology, 1*, 284–291.

Eysenck, S. B. G., and Long, F. Y. (1986). A cross-cultural comparison of personality in adults and children: Singapore and England. *Journal of Personality and Social Psychology, 50*, 124–130.

Feinstein, B. E. S., and Ward, C. (1990). Loneliness and psychological adjustment of sojourners: New perspective on culture shock. In D. M. Keats, D. Munro, and L. Mann (eds.), *Heterogeneity in cross-cultural psychology*. Lisse, Netherlands: Swets and Zeitlinger.

Feldman, R. (1968). Responses to compatriots and foreigners who seek assistance, *Journal of Personality and Social Psychology, 10*, 202–214.

Festinger, L. (1957). *A theory of cognitive dissonance*. Stanford: Stanford University Press.

Fishbein, M., and Ajzen, I. 1972. Attitudes toward objects as predictive of single and multiple behavioral criteria. *Psychological Review, 81*, 59–74.

Flack, M. J. (1976). Results and effects of study abroad. *The Annals of the American Academy of Political and Social Sciences, 424*, 107–117.

Fraczek, A. (1985). Moral approval of aggressive acts: A Polish-Finnish comparative study. *Journal of Cross-Cultural Psychology , 16*, 41–54.

Frager, R. (1970). Conformity and anti-conformity in Japan. *Journal of Personality and Social Psychology, 15*, 203–210.

Frideres, J. S., ed. (1989). *Multiculturalism and Intergroup Relations*. New York: Greenwood Press.

Fried, S. B., Gumpper, D. C., and Allen, J. C. (1973). Ten years of social psychology: Is there a growing commitment to field research? *American Psychologist, 28*, 155–156.

Furnham, A., and Bochner, S. (1982). Social difficulties in a foreign culture: An empirical analysis of culture shock. In S. Bochner (ed.), *Cultures in Contact: Studies in Cross-Cultural Interaction*. Oxford: Pergamon Press.

Furnham, A., and Bochner, S. (1986). *Culture Shock: Psychological Reactions to Unfamiliar Environments*. London: Methuen.

Gabrenya, W. K., Jr., Latané, B., and Wang, Y. E. (1983). Social loafing in cross-cultural perspective: Chinese in Taiwan. *Journal of Cross-Cultural Psychology, 14*, 368–384.

Gabrenya, W. K., Jr., Wang, Y. E., Latané, B. (1985). Social loafing on an optimizing task: Cross-cultural differences among Chinese and Americans. *Journal of Cross-Cultural Psychology, 16*, 223–242.

Garbarino, J., and Bronfenbrenner, U. (1976). The socialization of moral judgment and behavior in a cross-cultural perspective. In T. Lickona (ed.), *Morality: A Handbook of Moral Development and Behavior*. New York: Holt, Rinehart and Winston.

Gardner, G. H. (1962). Cross-cultural communication. *Journal of Social Psychology, 58*, 241–256.

Gardner, R.C. (1973). Ethnic stereotypes: The traditional approach, a new look. *Canadian Psychologist, 14*, 133–148.

Geertz, C. (1975). On the nature of anthropological understanding. *American Scientist, 63*, 47–53.

Gergen, K. J., and Gergen, M. M. (1974). Understanding foreign assistance through public opinion. *Yearbook of World Affairs, 28*, 125–140.

Gergen, K. J., Morse, S. J., and Bode, K. A. (1974). Overpaid or overworked? Cognitive and behavioral reactions to inequitable rewards. *Journal of Applied Social Psychology, 4*, 259–274.

Gergen, K. J., Morse, S. J., and Gergen, M. M. (1980). Behavior exchange in cross-cultural perspective. In H. C. Triandis and R. W. Brislin (eds.), *Handbook of Cross-Cultural Psychology. vol5: Social Psychology*. Boston: Allyn and Bacon.

Glazer, N., and Moynihan, D. P. (1970). *Beyond the melting pot*. Cambridge, Mass.: MIT Press.

Gorer, G. (1968). Man has no "killer" instinct. In M. F. A. Montagu (ed.), *Man and Aggression*, 27–36. New York: Oxford University Press.

Gouldner, A. (1960). The norm of reciprocity: A preliminary statement. *American Sociological Review, 25*, 161–179.

Greenberg, J. (1978). Equity, equality and the Protestant ethic: Allocating rewards following fair and unfair competition. *Journal of Experimental Social Psychology, 14*, 217–226.

Gregg, G. S. (1990). Underdevelopment in a North African tribe: Towards a psychology of peripheral social orders. *Journal of Social Issues, 46*, 71–92.

Grove, C. L., and Torbiorn, I. (1986). A new conceptualization of intercultural adjustment and the goals of learning. In R. M. Paige (ed.), *Cross-Cultural Orientation: New Conceptualizations and Applications*, 71–109. Chicago: University of Chicago Press.

Gudykunst, W. B., and Ting-Toomey, S. (1988). *Culture and Interpersonal Communication*. Newbury Park, Calif.: SAGE.

Gudykunst, W. B., and Hammer, M. R. (1988). Strangers and hosts: An extension of uncertainty reduction theory to intercultural adaptation. In Y. Y. Kim and W. B. Gudykunst (eds.), *Cross-Cultural Adaptation*. Newbury Park, Calif.: Sage.

Gullahorn, J. E., and Gullahorn, J. T. (1963). An extension of the U-curve hypothesis. *Journal of Social Issues, 19*, 33–47.

Gupta, U., and Singh, P. (1982). Exploratory studies in love and liking and types of marriages. *Indian Journal of Applied Psychology, 19*, 92–97.

Guthrie, G. M. (1975). A behavioral analysis of culture learning. In R. W. Brislin, S. Bochner, and W. J. Lonner (Eds.), *Cross-Cultural Perspectives on Learning*, New York: Wiley.

Hamilton, D. L., and Rose, T. L. 1980. Illusory correlation and the maintenance of sterotypic beliefs. *Journal of Personality and Social Psychology, 39,* 832–845.

Hammer, M. R. (1987). Behavioral dimensions of intercultural effectiveness: A replication and extension. *International Journal of Intercultural Relations, 11,* 65–88.

Hannigan, T. P. (1990). Traits, attitudes, and skills that are related to intercultural effectiveness and their implications for cross-cultural training: A review of the literature. *International Journal of Intercultural Relations, 14,* 89–111.

Harris, P. R., and Moran, R. T. (1979). *Managing cultural differences.* Houston, Tex.: Gulf.

Harré, R. (1984). *Personal Being: A Theory of Individual Behavior.* Cambridge: Harvard University Press.

Harré, R., Clarke, D. M., and De Carlo, N. (1985). *Motive and Mechanisms: An Introduction to the Psychology of Action.* London: Methuen.

Harré, R., and Muhlhausler, P. (1990). *Pronouns and People.* Oxford: Blackwell.

Hawes, F., and Kealey, D. J. (1981). An empirical study of Canadian technical assistants. *International Journal of Intercultural Relations, 5,* 239–258.

Hearnshaw, L. S. (1987). *The Shaping of Modern Psychology.* London: Routledge and Kegan Paul.

Herkovits, M. J. (1955). *Man and His Works: The Science of Cultural Anthropology.* New York: Alfred K. Knopf.

Hewstone, M., Stroebe, W., Codol, J. P., and Stephenson, G. M. (eds.) (1988). *Introducing Social Psychology.* Oxford: Blackwell.

Higbee, K. L., and Wells, M. G. (1972). Some research trends in social psychology during the 1960s. *American Psychologist, 27,* 963–966.

Hofstede, G. (1980). *Culture's Consequences.* Beverly Hills, Calif.: Sage.

Hogan, R. T., and Elmer, N. P. (1978). The biases of contemporary social psychology. *Social Research, 45,* 478–534.

Hong, G. Y. (1992). *Contributions of "Culture-Absent" Cross-Cultural Psychology to Mainstream Psychology.* Paper presented at Annual Meeting of Society for Cross-Cultural Research, Santa Fe.

Hsu, F. (1971). Filial piety in Japan and China. *The Journal of Comparative Family Studies, 2,* 67–74.

Hsu, F. L. K. (1983). *Rugged Individualism Reconsidered.* Knoxville: University of Tennessee Press.

Hui, C. H., and Triandis, H. (1986). Individualism-collectivism: A study in cross-cultural research. *Journal of Cross-Cultural Psychology, 17,* 225–248.

Innes, J. M. (1974). The semantics of asking a favour: An attempt to replicate cross-culturally. *International Journal of Psychology, 9,* 57–61.

Iwao, S. (1988). *Social Psychology's Model of Social Behavior: Is It Not Time for*

West to Meet the East? Paper presented at the 24th International Congress of Psychology, Sydney, Australia.

Jahoda, G. (1985). Theoretical and systematic approaches in cross-cultural psychology. In H. Triandis and W. W. Lambert (eds.), *Handbook of Cross-Cultural Psychology*. vol. 1, 69–141. Boston: Allyn & Bacon.

Jones, E. E., and Davis, K. E. 1965. From acts to dispositions: The attribution process in person perception. In L. Berkowitz (ed.), *Advances in Experimental Social Psychology*, vol 2., 220-256. New York: Academic Press.

Jones, R., and Popper, R. (1972). Characteristics of Peace Corps host countries and the behavior of volunteers. *Journal of Cross Cultural Psychology, 18*, 68–87.

Kâgitçibasi, Ç. (1978). Cross-cultural encounters: Turkish students in the United States. *International Journal of Intercultural Relations, 2*, 141–159.

Kagitcibasi, C. (1984). Socialization in traditional society: A challenge to psychology. *International Journal of Psychology, 19*, 145–157.

Kahle, L. R., and Beatty, S. E. (1987). Cognitive consequences of legislating postpurchase behavior: Growing up with the bottle bill. *Journal of Applied Social Psychology, 17*, 828–843.

Kandel, D. B. (1978). Similarity in real-life adolescent friendship pairs. *Journal of Personality and Social Psychology, 31*, 306–388.

Kandel, D. B. (1978). Similarity in real-life adolescent pairs. *Journal of Personality and Social Psychology, 31*, 306–311.

Kashima, Y., and Triandis, H. C. (1986). The self-serving bias in attributions as a coping strategy: A cross-cultural study. *Journal of Cross-Cultural Psychology, 17*, 83–97.

Katz, D., and Braly, K. (1935). Racial prejudice and racial stereotypes. *Journal of Abnormal and Social Psychology, 30*, 175–193.

Katz, I. (1981). *Stigma: A Social Psychological Analysis*. Hillsdale, N.J.: Erlbaum.

Kealey, D., and Ruben, B. D. (1983). Cross-cultural personnel selection: Criteria, issues and methods. In D. Landis and R. Brislin (eds.), *Handbook of Intercultural Training*. vol. 1. New York: Pergamon Press.

Keesing, R. M. (1974). Theories of culture. *Annual Review of Anthropology, 3*, 73–97.

Kelley, H. H. (1973). The process of causal attribution. *American Psychologist, 28*, 107–128.

Kidder, L. H., and Judd, C. M. (1986). *Research methods in social relations*. New York: Holt, Rinehart and Winston.

Kilham, W., and Mann, L. (1974). Level of destructive obedience as a function of transmitter and executant roles in the Milgram obedience paradigm. *Journal of Personality and Social Psychology, 29*, 696–702.

Kim, Y. (1978). A communication approach to the acculturation process: A study of Korean immigrants in Chicago. *International Journal of Intercultural relations, 2,* 197–224.

Kinder, D. M. (1986). The continuing American Dilemma: White resistance to racial change 40 years after Myrdal. *Journal of Social Issues, 42,* 151–172.

King, M., and Ziegler, M. (1975). *Research projects in Social Psychology: An Introduction in Methods.* Monterey, Calif.: Brooks/Cole.

Klineberg, O., and Hull, F. (1979). *At a Foreign University.* New York: Praeger.

Klineberg, O. (1981). The role of international university exchanges. In S. Bochner (ed.), *The Mediating Person: Bridges Between Cultures.* Boston: G.K. Hall.

Kohls, L. R. (1979). *Survival Kit for Overseas Living.* Chicago: Intercultural Network/SYSTRAN.

Kohn, M. L. (1969). *Class and Conformity: A Study in Values.* Homewood, Ill.: Dorsey.

Komarovsky, M. (1964). *Blue Collar Marriage.* New York: Random House.

Kumar, U. (1988). Mother-in-law, son, and daughter-in-law: A developmental analysis of the relationship in Hindu social context. In L. L. Adler (ed.), *Cross-Cultural Research in Human Development.* New York: Preager.

Lagerspetz, K., and Westman, M. (1980). Moral Approval of aggressive acts: A preliminary investigation. *Aggressive Behavior, 6,* 119–130.

Lambert, W. E. (1987). The fate of old-country values in a new land: A cross-cultural study of child reasoning. *Canadian Psychologist, 28,* 9–20.

Lambert, W. E., Moghaddam, F. M., Sorin, J., and Sorin, S. (1990). Assimilation vs. multiculturalism: Views from a community in France. *Sociological Forum, 5,* 387–411.

Lambert, W. E., and Taylor, D. M. (1990). *Coping with Cultural and Racial Diversity in Urban America.* New York: Praeger.

Lambert, W. W. (1971). Cross-cultural background to personality development and the socialization of aggression: Findings from the six culture study. In W. W. Lambert and R. Weisbrod (eds.), *Comparative Perspectives on Social Psychology,* 49–61. Boston: Little, Brown And Co.

Lambley, P. (1973). Authoritarianism and prejudice in South African student samples. *Journal of Social Psychology, 91,* 341–342.

Landis, D., and Brislin, R. W. (1983). *Handbook of Intercultural Training.* vols. 1, 2, and 3. New York: Pergamon.

L'Armand, K., and Pepitone, A. (1975). Helping to reward another person: A cross-sutural analysis. *Journal of Personality and Social Psychology, 31,* 189–198.

Latané, B., Williams, K, and Harkins, S. (1979). Many hands make light the work: Causes and consequences of social loafing. *Journal of Personality and Social Psychology, 37,* 822–832.

Leslie, G. R. (1967). *The Family in Social Context.* New York: Oxford University Press.

Leung, K. (1988). Theoretical advances in justice behavior: Some cross-cultural inputs. In M. H. Bond (ed.) *The Cross-Cultural Challenge to Social Psychology.* Newbury Park, Calif.: Sage.

Leung, K., and Bond, M. H. (1984). The impact of cultural collectivism on reward allocation. *Journal of Personality and Social Psychology, 47,* 793–804.

Leventhal, G. S. (1976). Fairness in social relations. In J. W. Thibaut, J. T. Spence, and R. C. Carlson (eds.), *Contemporary Topics in Social Psychology,* 211–239. Morristown, N.J.: General Learning Press.

LeVine, R., and Campbell, D. (1972). *Ethnocentrism.* New York: Wiley.

Lewicki, P. (1982). Social psychology as viewed by its practitioners: Survey of SESP members' opinions. *Personality and Social Psychology Bulletin, 3,* 409–416.

Lipman, W. (1922). *Public Opinion.* New York: Harcourt, Brace.

Locke, S. A., and Peinsod, F. M. (1982). Psychological preparation for young adults traveling abroad. *Adolescence, 17,* 815–819.

Lujansky H., and Mikula, G. (1983). Can equity theory explain the quality and stability of romantic relationships? *British Journal of Social Psychology, 22,* 101–112.

Maccoby, N. (1980). Promoting positive health behaviors in adults. In L. A. Bond and J. C. Rosen (eds.), *Competence and Coping During Adulthood.* Hanover, N.H.: University Press of New England.

Mackenzie, M. (1977). The deviant art of tourists: Airport art. In B. Farrell (ed.), *The Social and Economic Impact of Tourism of Pacific Communities.* Center for South Pacific Studies, University of California, Santa Cruz.

Mackie, M. (19730. Ethnic stereotypes, prejudicial attitudes, and education. *The Alberta Journal of Educational Research, 20,* 279–292.

Madsen, M. C., and Shapiro, A. (1970). Cooperative and competetive behavior of urban Afro-American, Anglo-American, Mexican-American and Mexican village children. *Developmental Psychology, 3,* 16–20.

Malpass, R. (1988). Why not cross-cultural psychology? A characterization of some mainstream views. In M. H. Bond (ed.) *The Cross-Cultural Challenge to Social Psychology.* Newbury Park, Calif.: Sage.

Mann, L. (1980). Cross-cultural studies in small groups. In H. C. Triandis and R. W. Brislin (eds.), *Handbook of Cross-Cultural Psychology. vol. 5: Social Psychology.* Boston: Allyn and Bacon.

Mantell, D. M. (1971). The potential for violence in Germany, *Journal of Social Issues, 27,* 101–112.

Marcus, H. R., and Kitayama, S. (1991). Culture and the self: Implications for cognition, emotion, and motivation. *Psychological Review, 98,* 224–253.

Matsuda, N. (1985). Strong, quasi-, and weak conformity among Japanese in the modified Asch procedure. *Journal of Cross-Cultural Psychology, 16,* 83–97.

Mazur, A. (1985). A biosocial model of status in face-to-face primate groups. *Social Forces, 64,* 377–402.

McDougall, W. (1908). *Introduction to Social Psychology.* London: Methuen.

McGuire, W. J. (1969). The nature of attitudes and attitude change. In G. Lindzey and E. Aronson (eds.), The Handbook of Social Psychology, vol. 3, 136–314. Reading, Mass.: Addison-Wesley.

Meeus, V. H. J., and Raaijmakers, Q. A. W. (1986). Administrative obedience: carrying out orders to use psychological-administrative violence. *European Journal of Social Psychology, 16,* 311–324.

Middlebrook, P. N. (1974). *Social Psychology and Modern Life.* New York: Alfred A. Knopf.

Mikula, G. (1974). Nationality, performance and sex as determinants of reward allocation. *Journal of Personality and Social Psychology, 29,* 435–440.

Milgram, S. (1961). Nationality and conformity. *Scientific America, 205,* 45–51.

Milgram, S. (1974). *Obedience to Authority: An Experimental View.* New York: Harper and Row, London: Tavistock.

Miller, A. G. (1973). Integration and acculturation of cooperative behavior among Blackfoot Indians and non-Indian Canadian children. *Journal of Cross-Cultural Psychology, 4,* 374–380.

Misra, G., ed. (1990). *Applied Social Psychology in India.* New Delhi: Sage.

Misumi, J. (1985). *The Behavioral Science of Leadership: An Interdisciplinary Japanese Research Program.* Ann Arbor: The University of Michigan Press.

Moghaddam, F. M. (1987). Psychology in the three worlds: As reflected by the crisis in social psychology and the move towards indigenous Third World psychology. *American Psychologist, 42,* 912–920.

Moghaddam, F. M. (1990). Modulative and generative orientations in psychology: Implications for psychology in the Three Worlds. *Journal of Social Issues, 46,* 21–41.

Moghaddam, F. M. and Taylor, D. M. (1985). Psychology in the developing world: An evaluation through the concepts of "dual perception" and "parallel growth. *American Psychologist, 40,* 1144–1146.

Moghaddam, F, M., and Taylor, D. M. (1986). What constitutes an "appropriate psychology" for the developing world? *International Journal of Psychology, 21,* 253–267.

Moghaddam, F. M., and Taylor, D. M. (1987). The meaning of multiculturalism for visible minority immigrant women. *Canadian Journal of Behavioural Science, 19,* 121–136.

Moghaddam, F. M., Taylor, D. M., and Lalonde, R. N. (1987). Individual and collective integration strategies among Iranians in Canada. *International Journal of Psychology, 22,* 301–313.

Moghaddam, F. M., Taylor, D. M., and Lalonde, R. N. (1989). Integration strategies and attitudes toward the built environment: A study of Haitian and Indian immigrant women in Montreal. *Canadian Journal of Behavioural Science, 21,* 160–173.

Moghaddam, F. M., and Solliday, E. A. (1991). "Balanced multiculturalism" and the challenge of peaceful coexistence in pluralistic societies. *Psychology and Developing Societies, 3,* 51–72.

Moghaddam, F. M., and Harre, R. (in press) The experimenter as dramatist. *American Behavioral Scientist.*

More, A. J. (1985). *Cultural and Value Differences Between Natives and Nonnatives: Some Intercultural Misunderstandings.* Paper presented to the Alberta Provincial Judges Association Program on Cross-Cultural Awareness. Lethbridge, Alberta, Canada.

Morsbach, H. (1977). The psychological importance of ritualized gift exchange in modern Japan. In S. A. Freed (ed.), Anthropology and the Climate of Opinion, *Annals of the New York Academy of Science, 292,* 221–226.

Morsbach, H. (1980). Major psychological factors influencing Japanese interpersonal relations. In N. Warren (ed.) *Studies in Cross-Cultural Psychology.* vol. 2, 317–344. London: Academic Press.

Moscovici, S. (1972). Society and theory in social psychology. In J. Israel and H. Tajfel (eds.), *The Context of Social Psychology,* 17–68. London: Academic Press.

Moscovici, S. (1985). Social influence and conformity. In G. Lindzey and E. Aronson (eds.), *The Handbook of Social Psychology.* vol. 2, 347–412. New York: Random House.

Munroe, R. L., and Munroe, R. H. (1975). *Cross-Cultural Human Development.* Monterey, Calif.: Brooks/Col Pub.

Munroe, R. L., Munroe, R. H., and Whiting, B. B. (eds.) (1981). *Handbook of Cross-Cultural Human Development.* Monterey, Calif.: Brooks/Cole.

Munroe, R. L., and Munroe, R. H. (1977). Cooperation and competition among East African and American children. *Journal of Social Psychology, 101,* 145-146.

Murdock, G. P. (1949). *Social Structure.* New York: Macmillan.

Murstein, B. I. (1974). *Love, Sex, and Marriage Through the Ages.* New York: Springer.

Mussen, P. H. (1977). *Roots of Caring, Sharing and Helping: The Development of Prosocial Behavior in Children.* San Francisco: W. H. Freeman.

Nakano, C. (1970). *Japanese Society.* Berkeley: University of California Press.

Nemeth, C. (1979). The role of an active minority in intergroup relations. In

W. G. Austin and S. Worshel (eds.), *The Social Psychology of Intergroup Relations.* Monterey, Calif.: Brooks/Cole.

Nemeth, C. J. (1986). Intergroup relations between majority and minority. In Worchel, S., and Austin, W. G. (eds.), *Psychology of Intergroup Relations,* 229–243. Chicago: Nelson-Hall.

Neuliep, J. W., and Hazelton, V. (1985). A cross-cultural comparison of Japanese and American persuasive strategy selection. *International Journal of Intercultural Relations, 9,* 389–404.

Newcomb, T. M. 1961. *The Acquaintance Process.* New York: Holt, Rinehart and Wilson.

Nicholson, N., Cole, S. G., and Rocklin, T. (1985). Conformity in the Asch situation: A comparison between contemporary British and U.S. university students. *British Journal of Social Psychology, 24,* 59–63.

Oberg, K. (1960). Culture shock: Adjusting to new cultural environments, *Practical Anthropology, 7,* 177–182.

O'Bryan, K. G., Reitz, J. G., and Kuplowska, O. (1976). *Non-official languages: A study in Canadian multiculturalism.* Ottawa, Canada: Minister Responsible for Multiculturalism, Government of Canada.

Olsak, S. (1983). Contemporary ethnic mobilization. *Annual Review of Sociology, 9,* 355–374.

Orpen, C. (1971). Authoritarianism and racial attitudes among English-speaking South Africans. *Journal of Social Psychology, 84,* 301–302.

Osgood, C. E. (1967). Cross-cultural comparability in attitude measurement via multilingual semantic differentials. In M. Fishbein (ed.), *Readings in Attitude Theory and Measurement.* New York: Wiley.

Ott, J. S. (1989). *The Organizational Culture Perspective.* Pacific Grove, Calif.: Brooks/Cole.

Paige, R. M. (1990). International students: Cross-cultural psychological perspectives. In R. W. Brislin (ed.), *Applied Cross-Cultural Psychology.* Newbury Park, Calif.: Sage.

Pearce, P. L. (1982). Tourists and their hosts: Some social and psychological effects of inter-cultural contact. In S. Bouchner (Ed.) *Cultures in Contact: Studies in Cross-Cultural Interaction.* Oxford: Pergamon.

Pettigrew, A. M. (1979). On studying organizational cultures. *Administrative Science Quarterly, 24,* 570–581.

Pettigrew, T. F. (1959). Regional differences in anti-Negro prejudice. *Journal of Abnormal and Social Psychology, 59,* 28–36.

Pettigrew, T. F. (1960). Social distance attitudes of South African students. *Social Forces, 38,* 246–253.

Pettigrew, T. F. (1988). Integration and pluralism. In P. A. Katz and D. A. Taylor (eds.), *Eliminating Racism: Profiles in Controversy.* New York: Plenum.

Petty, R. E., and Calioppo, J. T. 1986. *Communication and Persuasion: Central and Peripheral Routes to Attitude Change.* New York: Springer-Verlag.

Piliavin, J. A., Dovidio, J. F., Gaertner, S. L., and Clarke, R. D., III (1981). *Emergency Intervention.* New York: Academic.

Pratkanis, A. R., and Aronson, E. (1992). *Age of Propaganda: The Everyday Use and Abuse of Persuasion.* New York: Freeman.

Pruitt, D. G. (1968). Reciprocity and credit building in a laboratory dyad. *Journal of Personality and Social Psychology, 8,* 143–147.

Pruitt, F. J. (1978). The adaptation of African students to American society. *International Journal of Intercultural Relations, 2,* 90–118.

Quattrone, G. A. (1986). On the perception of a group's variability. In S. Worchel and W.G. Austin (eds.), *Psychology of Intergroup Relations,* 2d ed., 25–48. Chicago:Nelson-Hall.

Reischauer, E. O. (1988). *The Japanese Today: Change and Continuity.* Cambridge: Harvard University Press.

Richardson, A. (1974). *British Immigrants and Australia: A Psychosocial Inquiry.* Canberra, Australia: Australian National University Press.

Ross, L. D. (1977). The intuitive psychologist and his short-comings: Distortions in the attribution proces. In L. Berkowitz (ed.), *Advances in Experimental Social Psychology,* vol. 10. New York: Academic Press.

Rotter, J. (1973). Internal-external locus of control scale. In J. P. Robinson and R. P. Shaver (eds.), *Measures of Social Psychological Attitudes.* Ann Arbor, Mich.: Institute for Social Research.

Sampson, E. E. (1975). On justice as equity. *Journal of Social Issues, 31,* 45–64.

Sampson, E. E. (1977). Psychology and the American Ideal. *Journal of Personality and Social Psychology, 35,* 767–783

Sampson, E. E. (1981). Cognitive psychology as ideology. *American Psychologist, 36*(7), 730–743.

Schachter, S., Nuttin, J., DeMonchaux, C., Maucorps, P. A., Osmer, D., Duijker, H., Rommatveit, R., and Israel, J. (1954). Cross-cultural experiments on threat and rejection. *Human Relations, 7,* 403–439.

Schafer, R. B., and Keith, P. M. (1980). Equity and depression among married couples. *Social Psychology Quarterly, 43,* 430–435.

Schein, E. H. (1985). *Organizational culture and leadership.* San Fransisco: Jossey-Bass.

Schweder, R. A., and Bourne, E. J. 1982. Does the concept of the person vary cross-culturally? In A. J. Marsalla and G. M. White (eds.), *Cultural Conceptions of Mental Health and Therapy.* Dordrecht, Holland: D. Reidel.

Schweder, R. A., and LeVine, R. A., eds. (1984). *Culture Theory: Essays on Mind, Self, and Emotion.* Cambridge: Cambridge University Press.

Searle, W., and Ward, C. (1990). The prediction of psychological and sociocultural adjustment during cross-cultural transitions, *International Journal of Intercultural Relations, 14,* 449–464.

Sears, D. (1986). College sophomores in the laboratory: Influences of a narrow data base on social psychology's view of human nature. *Journal of Personality and Social Psychology, 51,* 515–530.

Segall, M. H. (1988). Cultural roots of aggressive behavior. In M. H. Bond (ed.), *The Cross-Cultural Challenge to Social Psychology,* 208–217. Newbury Park, Calif.: Sage.

Sellitiz, C., and Cook, S. W. (1962). Factors influencing attitudes of foreign students towards host country. *Journal of Social Issues, 18,* 7–23.

Sethi, S. P. (1975). *Japanese Business and Social Conflict: A Comparative Analysis of Response Patterns with American Business.* Cambridge, Mass.: Ballinger.

Seymour, S. (1981), Cooperation and competition: Some views and problems in cross-cultural analysis. In R. H. Monroe, R. L. Monroe and B. B. Whiting (eds.), *Handbook of Cross-Cultural Development,* 717–738. New York: Garland STPM Press.

Shanab, M. E., and Yahya, K.A. (1977). A behavioral study of obedience in children. *Journal of Personality and Social Psychology, 35,* 530–536.

Shanas, E. (1979). The family as a social support system in old age. *The Gerontologist, 19,* 169–174.

Shapira, A., and Madsen, M. (1969). Cooperative and competitive behavior of kibbutz and urban children in Isreal. *Child Development, 40,* 609–617.

Shapira, A., and Madsen, M. (1974). Between and within group cooperation and competition among kibbutz and non-kibbutz children. *Developmental Psychology, 10,* 140–145.

Sharma, M. P., and Jung, L. B. (1985). How cross-cultural social participation affects the international attitudes of U.S. students. *International Journal of Intercultural Relations, 9,* 377–387.

Sherif, M. (1937). An experimental approach to the study of attitudes. *Sociometry, 1,* 90–98.

Sherif, M. (1966). *Group Conflict and Cooperation: Their Social Psychology.* London: Routledge and Kegan Paul.

Simard, L. M. (1981). Cross-cultural interaction: Potential invisible barriers. *Journal of Social Psychology, 113,* 171–192.

Sinha, D. (1977). Some social disadvantages and development of certain perceptual skills. *Indian Journal of Psychology, 52,* 115–132.

Sinha, D. (1986). *Psychology in a Third World Country: The Indian Experience.* New Delhi: Sage.

Sinha, D., and Holtzman, W. H., eds. (1984). The impact of psychology on Third World development. *International Journal of Psychology, 19,* 3–192.

Sinha, J. B. P. (1980). *Nurturant Task Leader.* New Delhi: Concept Publishing Company.

Sinha, J. B. P. (1990). Role of psychology in national development. In G. Misra (ed.), *Applied Social Psychology in India* (pp.171–199). New Delhi: Sage.

Sommerland, E., and Bellingham, W. P. (1972). Cooperation-competition: A comparison of Australian, European, and Aboriginal school children. *Journal of Cross-Cultural Psychology, 3,* 149–157.

Stack, C. (1974). Sex roles and survival strategies in an urban Black community. In M. Z. Rosaldo and L. Lamphere (eds.), *Women, Culture and Society* (pp. 113–128). Stanford: Stanford University Press.

Steinkalk, E., and Taft, R. (1979). The effect of planned intercultural experience on the attitudes and behavior of the participants. *International Journal of Intercultural Relations, 3,* 187–197.

Stenning, B. W. (1979). Problems in cross-cultural contact: A literature review. *International Journal of Intercultural Relations, 3,* 269–313.

Taft, R. (1977). Coping with unfamiliar cultures. In N. Warren (ed.) *Studies in Cross-Cultural Psychology.* vol. 1, 121–153. London: Academic Press.

Tajfel, H. 1972. Experiments in a vacuum. In J. Israel and H. Tajfel (eds.), *The Context of Social Psychology.* London: Academic Press.

Tajfel, H., ed. (1984). *The Social Dimension.* 2 vols. Cambridge: Cambridge University Press.

Tajfel, H., and Fraser, C. eds. (1978). *Introducing Social Psychology.* Harmondsworth, U.K.: Penguin.

Taylor, D. M. (1990). *Carving a New Identity: The Role of Language in Education of Inuit Children in Arctic Quebec.* Montreal, Canada: Kativik School Board.

Taylor, D. M. (1991). The social psychology of racial and cultural diversity: Issues of assimilation and multiculturalism. In A. G. Reynolds (ed.), *Bilingualism,* Multiculturalism and Second-Language Learning. Hillsdale, N.J.: Lawrence Erlbaum.

Taylor, D. M. and Jaggi, V. (1974). Ethnocentrism in a south Indian context. *Journal of Cross-Cultural Psychology, 5,* 162–172.

Taylor D. M., and Brown, R. J. (1979). Towards a more social social psychology? *British Journal of Social and ClinicalPsychology, 18,* 173–180.

Taylor, D. M., and Simard, L. M. (1979). Ethnic identity and intergroup relations. In D. J. Lee (Ed.), *Emerging ethnic boundaries.* Ottawa: University of Ottawa Press.

Taylor, D. M., Doria, J., and Tyler, J. K. (1983). Group performance and cohesiveness: An attribution analysis. *Journal of Social Psychology, 119,* 187–198.

Taylor, D. M., and Lalonde, R. N. (1987). Ethnic stereotypes: A psychological analysis. In L. Driedger (ed.), *Ethnic Canada: Identities and Inequalities.* Toronto: Copp, Clark, Pittman.

Taylor, D. M., and Moghaddam, F. M. (1987). *Theories of Intergroup Relations: International Social Psychological Perspectives.* New York: Praeger.

Taylor, D. M., and Wright, S. C. (1990). Language attitudes in a multilingual northern community. *Canadian Journal of Native Studies, 9,* 85–119.

Teagues, B. W. (1976). *Selecting and Orienting Staff for Service Overseas.* New York: The Conference Board, Inc.

Tedeschi, J. T. (1988). How does one describe a Platypus? An outsider's questions for cross-cultural psychology. In M. H. Bond (ed.) *The Cross-Cultural Challenge to Social Psychology.* Newbury Park, Calif.: Sage.

Thibaut, J. W., and Kelley, H. H. (1959). *The Social Psychology of Groups.* New York: Wiley.

Thomas, D. (1975). Cooperation and competition among Polynesian and European children. *Child Development, 46,* 948–953.

Timaeus, E. (1968). Untersuchungen zum sogenannten konformen Verhatten. *Zeitschrift fur Experimentelle und Angewandte Psychologie, 15,* 176–194.

Ting-Toomey, S. (1986). Interpersonal ties in intergroup communication. In W. B. Gudykunst (ed.), *Intergroup Communication.* London: Edward Arnold.

Torbiorn, I. (1982). *Living Abroad: Personal Adjustment and Personnel Policy in the Overseas Setting.* Chichester, U.K.: Wiley.

Triandis, H. (1972). *The Analysis of Subjective Culture.* New York: Wiley.

Triandis, H. (1988). Collectivism vs. individualism: A reconceptualizatiion of a basic concept in cross-cultural psychology. In C. Bagley and G. K. Verma (eds.), *Personality, Cognition and Values: Cross-Cultural Perspectives in Childhood and Adolescence,* 60-95. London: Macmillan.

Triandis, H. (1990). Theoretical concepts that are applicable to the analysis of ethnocentrism. In R. W. Brislin (ed.), *Applied Cross-Cultural Psychology.* Newbury Park, Calif.: Sage.

Triandis, H. C., and Berry, J. W. (1980). *Handbook of Cross-Cultural Psychology.* vol.2. Boston: Allyn and Bacon.

Triandis, H., Bontempo, R., Villareal, M. J., Asai, M., and Lucca, N. (1988). Individualism and collectivism: Cross-cultural perspectives on self-in-group relationships. *Journal of Personality and Social Psychology, 54,* 323–338.

Trimble, J. F., and Richardson, S. S. (1982). Locus of control measures among American Indians: Cluster structure analytic characteristics. *Journal of Cross-Cultural Psychology, 13,* 228–238.

Turner, L., and Ash, J. (1975). *The Golden Hordes.* London: Constable.

Urbanowicz, C. (1978). Tourism in Tonga: Troubled times. In V. Smith (ed.), *Hosts and Guests.* Oxford: Blackwell.

Urbanowicz, C. (1977). Integrating tourists with other industries in Tonga. In B. Farrell (ed.), *The Social and Economic Impact of Tourism of Pacific Communities.* Center for South Pacific Studies, University of California, Santa Cruz.

Van den Broucke, S., DeSoete, G., and Bohrer, A. (1989). Free-response self-descriptions as a predictor of success and failure in adolescent exchange students, *International Journal of Intercultural Relations, 13,* 73–91.

Van Leeuwen, M. M. (1978). A cross-cultural examination of psychological differentiation in males and females. *International Journal of Psychology, 13,* 87–122.

Wagatsuma, H. (1973). Some problems of interracial marriage for the Japanese. In I. R. Stuart and L. E. Abt (eds.), *Interracial Marriages: Expectations and Relations,* 249–264. New York: Grossman.

Walsh, J. (1973). *Intercultural Education for the Community of Man.* Honolulu: University of Hawaii Press.

Walster, E., Walster, G. W., and Berscheid, E. (1978). *Equity, Theory and Research.* Boston: Allyn and Bacon.

Weary, G. (1979). Self-serving attributional biases: Perceptual or response distortions? *Journal of Personality and Social Psychology, 37,* 1418–1420.

Weiner, B., Freize, I,., Kukla, A., Reed, L., Rest, S., and Rosenbaum, R. M. (1971). In E. E. Jones, D. E. Kanouse, H. H. Kelley, R. E. Nisbett, S. Valins, and B. Weiner (eds.), *Attribution: Perceiving the Cause of Behavior,* 95–120. Morristown, N.J.: General Learning Press.

Weiner, N., Pandey, J., and Latané, B. (1981). *Individual and Group Productivity in the United States and India.* Paper presented at the annual meeting of the American Psychological Association, Los Angeles, Calif.

Weisz, J. R., Rothbaum, F. M., and Blackburn, T. C. (1984). Standing out and standing in: The psychology of control in America and Japan. *American Psychologist, 39,* 955–969.

Wheeler, L., and Reis, H. (1988). On titles, citations, and outlets: What do mainstreamers want? In M. H. Bond (ed.), *The Cross-Cultural Challenge to Social Psychology,* 36–40. Newbury Park: Sage.

Whiting, B. B., ed. (1963). *Six Cultures: Studies of Child Rearing.* Cambridge: Harvard University Press.

Whiting, B. B. (1965). Sex identity conflict and physical violence: A comparative study. *American Anthropologist, 67,* 123–140.

Whiting, B. B., and Edwards, C. P. (1988). *Children of Different Worlds: The Foundation of Social Behavior.* Cambridge: Harvard University Press.

Whiting, B. M., and Whiting, J. W. (1975). *Children of Six Countries: A Psychological Analysis.* Cambridge: Harvard University Press.

Whittaker, J. O., and Meade, R. D. (1967). Social pressure in the modification and distortion of judgement: A cross-cultural study. *International Journal of Psychology, 2,* 109–113.

Wilke, H., and Steur, T. (1972). Overpayment: Perceived qualifications and financial compensation. *European Journal of Social Psychology, 2,* 273–284.

Witkin, H. A., and Berry, J. W. (1975). Psychological differentiation in cross-cultural perspective. *Journal of Cross-Cultural Psychology, 6,* 4–87.

Witkin, H. A., Lewis, H. B., Hertzman, M., Machover, K., Meissner, P. B., and Wapner, S. (1954). *Personality Through Perception*. New York: Harper and Row.

Witkin, H. A., Dyk, R. B., Faterson, H. F., Goodenough, D. R., and Karp, S. A. (1962). *Psychological Differentiation*. New York: Wiley.

Yu, L. C. (1983). Patterns of filial beliefs and behavior within the contemporary Chinese-American family. *International Journal of Sociology of the Family, 13,* 17–36.

Yu, L. C. and Wu, S. (1988). Effects of length of stay in the United States on how the Chinese fulfilled their filial obligations. In L. L. Adler (ed.), *Cross-Cultural Research in Human Development*. New York: Praeger.

Zimbardo, P. G. (1972). Pathology of imprisonment. *Transactional/Society,* 4–8 (a).

Zimbardo, P. G. (1973). The mind is a formidable jailer: A Pirandellian prison. *The New York Times,* April 8, p. 38.

Author Index

Subject Index